W9-CAR-987

ADD AND THE
COLLEGE STUDENT

ADD
AND THE
COLLEGE
STUDENT

A Guide for
High School and College Students
with
Attention Deficit Disorder

◆ ◆ ◆

PATRICIA O. QUINN, M.D.
Editor

MAGINATION PRESS • NEW YORK

371.93
A222
cc L
6/94
13.95

Library of Congress Cataloging-in-Publication Data

ADD and the college student : a guide for high school and college
students with attention deficit disorder / Patricia O. Quinn,
editor.
    p.   cm.
  ISBN 0-945354-58-4
  1. Attention-deficit-disordered youth – Education (Higher) – United
States. 2. Attention-deficit-disordered youth – Education
(Secondary) – United States. 3. College student orientation – United
States. I. Quinn, Patricia O.
LC4713.4.A33   1993
371.93 – dc20   93-36668
                                                     CIP

Copyright © 1994 by Patricia O. Quinn

Cover photograph by Sandy Kavalier © Patricia O. Quinn

All rights reserved. No part of this book may be
reproduced by any process whatsoever without the written
permission of the copyright owner.

Published by
MAGINATION PRESS
an Imprint of Brunner/Mazel, Inc.
19 Union Square West
New York, NY 10003
1-800-825-3089

Manufactured in the United States of America

10 9 8 7 6 5 4 3 2

*This book is dedicated to my son, Tim,
who with hard work has successfully made it this
far despite his ADD. You have shown me all of the positive
qualities that go along with the deficits. I am
very proud of you.*

POQ

CAMBRIA COUNTY LIBRARY
JOHNSTOWN, PA. 15901

Table of Contents

Preface

The transition from high school to college and from family to semi-independent living can be difficult for some students. If the student has Attention Deficit Disorder (ADD), this transition can not only be difficult but can cause stress unless the special concerns are understood and handled properly. This stress can be experienced by both the student and the family.

The authors of *ADD and the College Student* help this student and his or her family learn how to make this transition successfully.

If a student has any disability, such as ADD, it is critical that he or she understand the disorder and the impact it has on school, family, and social life. This student must know what ADD is, how it effects all aspects of life, and what needs to be done to treat, compensate for, or accommodate for the problems. Without this knowledge, the student cannot be successful as his or her own advocate. ADD may prevent him or her from performing up to true potential.

Each chapter in this book helps the individual student and his or her parents learn about ADD, its impact, and approaches to treatment. The focus is on special issues that have to be handled from the last year of high school through the transition into the early years of college.

To succeed in college, parents need to know how to seek out the right professionals to help and the best colleges to consider. The student with ADD must have the understanding that leads to being an assertive self-advocate. This book will help the student and his or her family successfully handle the challenges of the transition into college.

Larry B. Silver, M.D.

Clinical Professor of Psychiatry
Director of Training in Child and
Adolescent Psychiatry
Georgetown University
School of Medicine
Washington, DC

About the Authors

Thomas Applin, M.D., has a private practice in child and adolescent psychiatry in Chevy Chase, Maryland, and is a member of the faculty of Georgetown University Medical Center. He is also a psychiatric consultant at Holy Trinity School in Georgetown. He was previously a staff child/adolescent psychiatrist at the Regional Institute for Children and Adolescents (RICA) in Rockville, Maryland.

Erik Benke is a senior at Georgetown University, Washington, DC. He is majoring in business with an emphasis on management. He is also pursuing studies at American University in audio engineering and plans to attend law school.

Elayne Clift, M.A., is a professional writer and health communication specialist with 20 years experience in the field of public health. She has been a social worker, program manager, and health educator with an emphasis on women's health, and has worked internationally on a variety of projects sponsored by USAID and UNICEF. Her most recent book is a collection of essays entitled *Telling It Like It Is: Reflections of a Not So Radical Feminist*. She is the recipient of several awards, including the New Jersey Education Association's 1992 Award for Excellence in Journalism.

Peter S. Latham and **Patricia Horan Latham** have been practicing law for over 25 years. They have authored two books, *Attention Deficit Disorder and the Law* and *Learning Disabilities and the Law.* They are founders of the first four-year college for students with learning disabilities. They have been active in learning disability and attention deficit disorder associations and have written and produced television programs on those topics. The Lathams recently founded the National Center for Law and Learning Disabilities to address legal issues of concern to individuals with learning disabilities and attention deficit disorders.

Bennett L. Lavenstein, M.D., is a pediatric neurologist in private practice in northern Virginia. He is the Director of Pediatric Neurology at the Fairfax Hospital for Children. He is also on the clinical faculty of Georgetown University Medical Center in the Department of Pediatrics and Child Neurology. Dr. Lavenstein serves on the medical advisory board of the Tourette's Syndrome Association. He is active in a number of neurologic associations devoted to neurology and child neurology.

Faith Leonard, Ph.D., is the Associate Director of the Center for Psychological and Learning Services, The American University, Washington, DC. She is also an adjunct faculty member in the School of Education.

Anne McCormick, M.Ed., is the Senior Learning Services Counselor at the Center for Psychological and Learning Services at the American University in Washington, DC, where she coordinated the program for students with learning disabilities at its inception eleven years ago.

Kathleen Nadeau, Ph.D., has practiced psychology in the Washington, DC, area since 1970. She is the cofounder of Chesapeake Psychological Services, which provides services in the areas of learning disabilities and attention deficit disorder, including support groups for children, adolescents, and adults. She is the author of a book for young children on ADHD entitled *Learning to Slow Down and Pay Attention.*

Kathleen O'Connor, Ph.D., is the founder and Executive Director of College Planning, a Rockville, Maryland–based educational counseling firm. Dr. O'Connor has been an educator, a high school guidance counselor, a college teacher, and a university administrator. She has been in private practice since 1981.

Patricia O. Quinn, M.D., is a developmental pediatrician who has practiced in the Washington, DC, area since 1972. She was formerly Director of Medicine at Georgetown University Child Development Center. She continues there as Clinical Assistant Professor of Pediatrics and Child Psychiatry. Dr. Quinn specializes in child development and psychopharmacology. In her private practice, she sees high-risk infants and young children and follows patients through their school years. Dr. Quinn works extensively in the areas of attention deficit disorder, hyperactivity, and learning disabilities. She gives workshops and has published widely in these fields, including *Putting on the Brakes: Young People's Guide to Understanding Attention*

Deficit Hyperactivity Disorder (ADHD) and *The "Putting on the Brakes" Activity Book for Young People with ADHD.*

Chris Willingham is a junior at Davidson College, Davidson, North Carolina, and is a political science major. In high school he was class president, played football and ran track, and became an Eagle Scout.

1.

WHAT IS ATTENTION DEFICIT DISORDER?

Patricia O. Quinn, M.D.

This is a book written for high school juniors and seniors and college students with attention deficit disorder (ADD). A number of experts have come together not only to discuss what ADD is about, but also to offer practical solutions to help you deal effectively with this disorder.

But first: What is ADD and how do you know that you have it?

ADD is a neurological condition that affects learning and behavior and occurs in approximately 5% to 10% of the population, depending on what scientific studies you read. It begins in childhood, and it was initially thought to be outgrown by adolescence. However, we now know that this is probably true for about only 40% to 60% of persons with ADD. Symptoms may not be as bothersome in adulthood, but they are still present to some degree.

Symptoms of the disorder may include attention deficits, impulsivity, hyperactivity, mood swings, low frustration tolerance, and difficulty falling asleep at night. Some people may daydream, some may have difficulty completing tasks, others may be disorganized and forgetful, or may procrastinate. Some may even find it difficult to concentrate on reading this book.

All of the symptoms of this disorder have an impact on academic performance, including performance in college. There may be problems with time management; initiating, maintaining or shifting focus; completing assignments on time; organizing; and setting priorities. These problems are often compounded by college living conditions. Finally, because college is more demanding than most prior schooling, methods of compensating for ADD that worked previously may not continue to be successful. It is often around the first semester break that the college student with ADD suddenly realizes that he or she is having problems.

Chapter 3 discusses the neurological basis and treatment of this condition. However, it is important to mention that ADD does not always occur alone, and that about 40% of individuals with ADD can also be learning disabled or have other problems, such as anxiety, depression, tics, Tourette's syndrome, or obsessive-compulsive disorder.

Why am I not referring to attention deficit hyperactivity disorder (ADHD) here? The reason is that the hyperactivity component of ADD is usually outgrown by early adolescence. However, both terms—ADD and ADHD—will be used throughout this book.

The person with attention deficits who is not hyperactive is usually not diagnosed for many years. That is why some of you are hearing about this disorder for the first time as young adults. Even if they have gone unrecognized, the problems have been there during your growing years. *Underachievement* may be the first signal to you and others that something is wrong. I bet you are all tired of hearing, "You could do better if you only tried harder" or "She is not working up to her potential."

Let's look at some of the symptoms of ADD.

Hyperactivity is usually seen now as physical restlessness. The student has difficulty staying seated, is always on the go, or is a restless sleeper. **Sleep disorders** are also seen. Commonly, these symptoms represent difficulty with the arousal system. The person with ADD needs little sleep, or has trouble falling asleep. Some people with ADD describe feeling as though they will fall asleep if they sit too long.

Mental restlessness and easy **distractibility** are also symptoms. These often involve changing from one topic or task to another or focusing on the less important aspects of a task. A distractible person has difficulty deciding the most important thing to be doing at a given moment. Should he or she continue to write that paper or play the guitar that is standing in the corner? Things may assume equal importance, such as the teacher lecturing and the man outside mowing the lawn.

Mood changes can be a hallmark of the adolescent and adult with ADD. He or she may be impatient or irritable. Temper outbursts or unpredictable behaviors are also seen. Sometimes people with ADD engage in physically daring activities. They are constantly being asked, "Why did you do that?"

Impulsivity can be best described as acting without thinking. In addition to impulsive behaviors, a person with ADD may talk too much, interrupt, not listen when others are speaking, or always need to have the last word.

Attention problems can also be seen in relationship to completing tasks or activities. Not only do people with ADD have difficulty completing tasks, but they may also have difficulty initiating them. This means procrastinating and leaving things to the last minute. The pressure of "being under the gun" or needing to get things done immediately is then used as the motivating factor. People with ADD may also find that they have difficulty shifting focus from one task to another or difficulty sustaining attention. This causes problems even with enjoyable tasks such as reading or watching movies.

Problems with time management are also evident. The person with ADD may always seem rushed or unprepared. **Disorganization** is a serious problem. This may lead to the person's frequently losing things or forgetting to do things.

Because of the frustration associated with the above symptoms of ADD, secondary symptoms of **depression** may also emerge, including irritability and negative thinking. A person with ADD may be very sensitive to rejection and may even withdraw socially. Some people make up for these feelings by becoming the class clown, which is simply a way of compensating for the difficulties they are experiencing.

Yet, having ADD does not have to be thought of as entirely negative. Many of its characteristics can be used positively. Excess energy can be channeled to accomplish a great deal. Persons with ADD can be very artistic and creative. However, in order to make the most of what they have, it is important for those with ADD to find just the right fit in college and to make wise career choices.

Addressing the issues that arise as a result of having ADD through a *total treatment program* is essential. Such a program usually includes the use of medication, individual therapy, learning accommodations, and support groups. Recognizing and dealing with the feelings related to having been diagnosed with ADD is a necessary step toward making positive decisions for your future.

Learning accommodations can help you achieve success and reach your potential academically, but career counseling is also important. Adults with ADD often experience job dissatisfaction and as a result change employment frequently. This can be avoided if informed choices are made and the right placement is found.

The following chapters will address all of these issues. Chapter 2 will help answer the question: How do you know if you have ADD? The questionnaire lists many of the symptoms of ADD. You may not identify with all of the symptoms, but recognizing some may help you understand better what you have been experiencing. Self-recognition and knowledge are the first steps, but diagnosing ADD is still a job for professionals. A multifactored evaluation is essential to determine if an individual has ADD. Diagnostic assessment should be made by a clinician or team of clinicians who have expertise and experience with ADD and its related conditions.

2.

HOW DO YOU KNOW IF YOU HAVE ADD?

Kathleen Nadeau, Ph.D.

Editor's note: This checklist is provided to help you evaluate various symptoms and gain a better self-awareness. It should *not* be used for "self-diagnosis." Specifically the ADHD Questionnaire is designed to be used as part of a multifactorial evaluation, which should include a structured interview with a counselor, a therapist, or a physician who has expertise in diagnosing ADHD. If you find that you are responding positively to a number of the items it is important to seek a professional assessment or discuss items of concern with your therapist.

POQ

COLLEGE-LEVEL ADHD QUESTIONNAIRE

Rate EVERY statement by placing the appropriate number that most fits how you feel about the statement in the space to the left of each item. If an item does not apply to you, write NA for "not applicable."

> 0 – I do not feel this statement describes me at all.
> 1 – I feel this statement describes me to a slight degree.
> 2 – I feel this statement describes me to a moderate degree.
> 3 – I feel this statement describes me to a large degree.
> 4 – I feel this statement describes me to a very large degree.

This questionnaire is meant to be used as a structured interview. Please feel free to write down additional comments about any item. If an item used to be true for you, but is no longer an issue, give two ratings for that item and circle the "past" rating (that is, if you drank heavily in high school, but are a moderate, social drinker now, you would mark the statement "I have used alcohol excessively" 2 ④). Any category in which most of your responses are 3s and 4s is an area of concern to discuss with your counselor or therapist.

INATTENTION

__4__ It is hard for me to stick to one thing for a long period of time (except TV, computer games, or socializing).

__4__ My parents have complained that I don't listen.

__4__ I tune in and out during class lectures.

__4__ It is hard for me to study for long periods of time.

__4__ Often when reading, my eyes scan the words, but my mind is somewhere else.

__4__ In group situations, I sometimes lose track of the conversation.

IMPULSIVITY

_4_ I "got in trouble" in school for talking or misbehaving.

_2_ I tend to "go with my feeling" and often don't think before I act.

_4_ I interrupt others in conversation.

_2_ Sometimes I hurt people's feelings without meaning to because I speak before I think.

_1_ I am a risk taker.

_2_ I make decisions quickly.

_3_ When I have a job to do, I just dive in and figure it out as I go.

HYPERACTIVITY

_4_ I eat quickly.

_2_ I need to move or exercise frequently.

_3_ Sometimes I bother people around me by tapping, jiggling, or moving.

_3_ I have trouble slowing down.

_4_ I am very talkative.

_4_ I often feel bored and impatient.

_4_ In class I feel restless and fidgety.

DISTRACTIBILITY

_4_ I become easily sidetracked.

_4_ I am constantly noticing or thinking of things unrelated to the task I am doing.

_4_ I jump from topic to topic in conversation.

_4_ It is hard for me to keep focused on long-term projects.

_4_ A 5-minute break from studying can easily become an hour-long break if I'm not careful.

_4_ If I don't do something when I think of it, I usually forget to do it later.

_4_ It is very hard for me to study if people are talking nearby.

HYPERFOCUSING

_3_ Sometimes I become so involved in what I'm doing that I completely lose track of time.

_2_ People talk to me or call me when I'm engrossed in something and I don't hear them.

TIME MANAGEMENT

_4_ I have trouble being "on time."

_4_ I tend to procrastinate.

3 I am unrealistic about how long a task will take.

2 I tend to make too many commitments.

N/A My girlfriend/boyfriend gets annoyed because I often keep her/him waiting.

4 No matter how good my intentions are, I end up doing "all-nighters" before exams, or when papers are due.

SELF-DISCIPLINE

4 I have difficulty sticking to my plans for "self-improvement."

4 I can't tear myself away from activities I like, even when I know I will be late for something.

4 I usually do what I like, and put off things that I ought to do.

4 The only way I can get myself to study is to wait until the deadline.

4 I have taken up and dropped many interests.

4 I have been called lazy.

2 I have been called irresponsible.

3 It is hard for me to stay in and study when friends invite me to go out.

SLEEP/AROUSAL PROBLEMS

3 I have very irregular sleep patterns.

3 Falling asleep at night has always been difficult for me.

_4_ I often oversleep.

_4_ Sitting in class or studying, I quickly feel tired, no matter how much sleep I got the night before.

_4_ I tend to fall asleep for catnaps if I sit down or lie down to relax.

ORGANIZATION/STRUCTURE

_2_ I rarely plan my day.

_4_ I tend to be messy.

_2_ My messiness has caused conflict with my parents or roommate.

_3_ I have trouble keeping up with several simultaneous projects.

_4_ I become overwhelmed when I have too many choices.

_4_ I have trouble managing money.

_4_ I have difficulty keeping my checkbook balanced.

_4_ I have had to borrow money from friends or parents because I was in a jam.

_4_ I try to get organized, but it never lasts long.

_2_ I often turn papers in late.

_3_ It's hard for me to prioritize things I need to do.

STIMULANTS

__4__ I drink four or more cups of coffee or cokes a day.

__2__ I use No-Doze or other stimulant pills to keep alert.

_N/A_ Smoking cigarettes helps me concentrate when I study.

SUBSTANCE ABUSE

__0__ I have used alcohol excessively.

__0__ My friends or parents have been concerned about my drinking.

__0__ I have used drugs recreationally.

__0__ I have experimented with hard drugs.

__0__ I have a substance addiction.

MEMORY

__3__ I tend to forget appointments.

__3__ I rely on parents, friends, girlfriends/boyfriends to be my reminder.

__4__ I tend to misplace personal items.

__1__ I lose my car keys.

__3__ I forget what my parents or others ask me to do.

3 It is hard for me to remember things I intend to do.

4 If I don't write it down, I'll forget it.

2 Even if I write things down, I often misplace the note.

FRUSTRATION TOLERANCE

4 I have been called impatient.

4 I become easily frustrated.

4 It is hard to tolerate people who do things slowly.

4 I hate to wait.

4 I tend to give up quickly if I can't figure out how to do something.

ANGER

2 I fought frequently as a child.

4 I have a short fuse.

3 If someone raises her or his voice at me, I yell back.

1 I have punched holes in walls or doors out of anger.

4 I usually become angry if I am criticized.

4 It is almost impossible for me to remain calm if someone is acting in an angry manner toward me.

EMOTIONAL LABILITY

4 I tend to be moody.

4 My feelings (positive or negative) are very intense.

3 I have "thin skin."

4 I have very intense premenstrual symptoms of moodiness and emotionality.

3 I tend to overreact.

4 I cry more often than my friends do.

1 As a child, I was teased for getting upset.

ACADEMICS

4 I have been called an underachiever.

4 School has seemed boring and frustrating for as long I can remember.

4 My grades went down in junior high compared to elementary school.

4 My siblings were better students than I was.

4 I was diagnosed with learning problems.

4 My teachers and parents always felt I was unmotivated in school.

_4_ My grades varied from As to Fs.

_1_ Low grades were often a result of not turning in homework.

_3_ Even when I studied hard for tests, during the exam I "blanked out" and couldn't remember information.

_4_ Careless errors have frequently lowered my grades.

ANXIETY/DEPRESSION

_4_ I have had periods when I felt depressed for weeks or months.

_4_ I have felt so anxious and overwhelmed that I feel like dropping out of school.

_3_ I worry a lot about my future.

_3_ I'm afraid I'll never "get my act together."

_3_ I have occasionally felt suicidal.

_1_ Often I drink or party just to get my mind off my troubles.

_4_ I have taken medication for anxiety or depression.

_4_ I have been in therapy.

_2_ Sometimes I can't get out of bed I feel so overwhelmed.

_3_ I have headaches, stomachaches, neckaches, or backaches from tension and worry.

SELF-ESTEEM AND CONFIDENCE

_3_ I tend to put myself down.

4 I try to avoid competitive situations.

4 I overreact to criticism.

4 I can't take being teased.

3 I worry a lot about making mistakes.

2 I am always "messing up."

OPPOSITIONAL TENDENCIES

2 I was a "difficult child."

4 I don't like being told what to do.

3 I argue a lot.

3 I have been called stubborn.

3 I have had many disagreements with my parents.

1 I have been fired or have had arguments with supervisors on jobs.

SOCIAL/INTERPERSONAL

1 I was teased a lot as a kid.

1 I had trouble getting along with other kids.

3 I always felt "different" as a child.

1 I have been called bossy.

2 Sometimes I am too blunt or critical.

N/A Though I don't mean to be, I have been called inconsiderate by my roommate or girlfriend/boyfriend.

1 I tend to have conflicts with roommates or co-workers.

FAMILY HISTORY

4 There is a history of alcoholism in my family.

4 There is a history of depression in my family.

N/A Other family members (including cousins, aunts, uncles) have been diagnosed as hyperactive or learning disabled.

2 One of my parents says he or she was a lot like me when they were younger.

3.

THE BIOCHEMISTRY OF ADD AND MEDICATION

Bennett L. Lavenstein, M.D.

Over the past several years, research has been directed toward understanding many conditions affecting the brain. However, no single defect in the brain has been found to explain the complex range of emotions, behaviors, and performance seen in different degrees in people with ADD. Symptoms of attention deficit disorder may be associated with various features of the brain. Identifying these associations and determining the cause of the distress related to brain function have been subjects of great interest and investigation. With recent advances in biology, neurology, and psychology, many pieces of information have become available to explain ADD. In the next few pages, we will explore some of the ideas relating to the neurobiology and treatment of ADD.

The frontal lobe has been suggested as a major area of the brain responsible for the features of ADD. Although controversy

19

exists as to what degree frontal lobe function is involved, its role in governing behavior and its responsibility for at least some of the symptoms are worth considering. Frontal lobe function may be associated with the ability to maintain serial or sequentially received information. It has also been associated with problems of vigilance or concentration. An inability to handle sequential or serial information is an important characteristic of ADD.

Frontal lobe function is also associated with motivation, interest, drive, and the ability to think ahead and anticipate future needs. Although a person's IQ may be average or above, the frontal lobe functions may not be utilized maximally, resulting in many of the symptoms seen in ADD. Frontal lobe function may also be responsible for controlling spontaneous activity.

There are also connections between the frontal lobes and other areas of the brain that play a significant role in expression of symptoms of ADD/ADHD. Deeply placed nuclei within the brain receive messages from the frontal lobe. Neuroimaging techniques have demonstrated that there may be a decreased metabolic activity of the brain tissue in these structures, with greater decrease in activity on the right side than on the left. Therefore, a difference in right hemisphere brain metabolic activity may explain the symptoms that some people experience.

Motor restlessness is a common symptom in patients with ADHD. A neurochemical basis has been postulated for this symptom, and studies have focused on the role of neurotransmitters. These substances (neurotransmitters) are produced, secreted, or stored within the central nervous system. Some neurotransmitters are dopamine, norepinephrine,

epinephrine, acetylcholine, and serotonin. Diverse symptoms such as depression, mania, sleep disorders, decreased attentiveness, underarousal, and overarousal have been related to neuronal connections and actions of neurotransmitters within the brain.

Dopamine may be decreased in the prefrontal brain nuclei and be responsible for motor restlessness. Improvement in restlessness and inattention has been found to correlate with increased levels of dopamine. Other substances, such as epinephrine, norepinephrine, acetylcholine, and serotonin, also play important roles in the regulation of alertness, attentiveness, sleeplessness, concentration, awareness, and retention of information being gathered by the brain.

Medications such as methylphenidate and dextroamphetamine may stimulate the effects of dopamine and other neurotransmitters to decrease restlessness, impulsiveness, and hyperactivity. These effects, in turn, may be responsible for improving concentration, restlessness, attentiveness, and impulsivity. A balance between inhibitory neurotransmitters—those that effectively produce a "calming" effect in the central nervous system—and the excitatory neurotransmitters may be responsible for the improvement seen in many behavioral and academic areas.

In the next few pages, we will focus on drug therapy of ADD and ADHD. Some of the drugs and agents discussed will be familiar, but many of the names may be new to you. There is no attempt in this section to prescribe one type of medication over another; only your physician can do that. However, the background information provided may enable you to discuss with your physician the type and dose of medication given.

PSYCHOSTIMULANTS

As a group, these agents have had a long history in the treatment of ADD and ADHD, with variable results. In fact, it was over 40 years ago that the first drugs, namely amphetamines, were used. Today, Dexedrine spansules are still popularly prescribed in appropriate dosages, and may be very effective. In addition, methylphenidate (Ritalin) and pemoline (Cylert) are used.

Methylphenidate (Ritalin) is perhaps the most commonly used of the group. It is available in several dosages, ranging from 5 mg to 20 mg. There is also a sustained-release form of the drug at a 20-mg strength. The regular form of the drug is absorbed within 30 minutes and lasts 4–6 hours. The sustained-released form may be absorbed in anywhere from 1.5 to 8 hours, but generally within 2 hours, and lasts 4–6 hours following absorption. The degree of absorption may vary from individual to individual, making the therapeutic effect more or less potent.

Some individuals become tolerant to the medication over time and require a dosage adjustment. Variation in weight (such as weight gain), additional stresses, or significant job or school pressures may all be associated with a need for change in dosage.

Stimulants can produce many side effects. Some are common, some uncommon, and others very rare. However, as with all medications, physicians prescribing these and the other drugs discussed below should fully discuss the potential effects with their patients. Weight loss, irritability, abdominal pain, insomnia, and mild social withdrawal are short-term effects. Overmedication can lead to slowness in mental task (cognitive) performance. Symptoms of tic disorder, depression, hyper-tension, and rapid heartbeat may occur. With pemoline (Cylert), abnormal liver function with chemical hepatitis may take place in up to 3% of individuals. Dizziness, nightmares, lethargy, fatigue, anxiety, fearfulness, rash, hives, and mild nonspecific complaints have all been associated with these agents.

Possible psychological dependence and addiction to stimulants has been studied, but *no* evidence demonstrating any increased incidence of these problems has been found. Many of the specific side effects listed above can be effectively managed by a change in dosage or a change in preparation by your physician.

TRICYCLIC ANTIDEPRESSANTS

These agents have proved useful in patients with ADHD. Although they may be less effective than the psychostimulants, because of their pharmacological action, they sometimes have additional beneficial effects and can be an excellent alternative. Both imipramine (Tofranil) and desipramine (Norpramin) have been extensively studied and used. Desipramine has less sedation and may be better tolerated, but because of possible cardiac rhythm disturbances, electrocardiograms must be done prior to the administration of these drugs and in follow-up to monitor for possible side effects.

Other tricyclic antidepressants include amitriptyline (Elavil), which is useful for the treatment of depression, school phobia, and panic disorder, and clomipramine (Anafranil), used for obsessive-compulsive disorder and undifferentiated attention deficit disorder. These agents have been used in the treatment of depression, but they also may be successful in the treatment of ADHD independent of their antidepressant effects. In fact, the blood levels used to monitor the concentration of these agents in the blood system, an important tool for their use in antidepression, are not necessary or even helpful in predicting success when used for ADHD.

Common side effects of the tricyclics include dry mouth, sedation, constipation, fast heart rate, and slowing of cardiac conduction. Serious cardiac effects have been noted in young children and older adults. Preexisting hypertension may be worsened. Occasionally, rash, tics, photosensitivity, or breast enlargement (gynecomastia) may occur. Monitoring of blood pressure, heart rate, cardiograms, and the like is important and should be carried out.

There are potential serious drug interactions when these agents are combined with alcohol, abusive substances, thyroid medications, oral contraceptives, lithium, barbiturates, and drugs containing sympathomimetic amines, which are commonly found in cold medications.

OTHER DRUGS

Fluoxetine (Prozac) is primarily an antidepressant but is gaining widespread use for a number of other conditions. It is not generally thought of as a primary agent in ADHD, but a physician may prescribe it when indicated.

Clonidine (Catapres) is primarily an antihypertensive agent. It was found in 1980 to be useful in several other conditions, including Tourette's syndrome, mania, ADHD, and aggression. It has also been used for migraine, nicotine withdrawal, and obsessive-compulsive disorder. Because of its action on the central nervous system, this drug may be very advantageous in certain patients who have a mixture of symptoms, for example, tics and ADD, thereby eliminating the need for multiple medications. In an overly aroused, aggressive individual, clonidine may be more beneficial than a psychostimulant. However, it is not effective on the distractibility of ADHD. Psychostimulants may be more effective in focusing attention, but clonidine may diminish arousal. This agent is associated with significant sedation, which means that to achieve a beneficial response, it may take 2–4 weeks to produce a therapeutic drug level that can be tolerated. As a minimum, 10 days is usually required to introduce the drug and achieve any effect. A prolonged form of the drug, clonidine skin patch, maintains a constant blood level for about five days and wears off in a week. The following side effects are commonly recognized with this agent: sedation, headache, dizziness, nausea, vomiting, depression, cardiac rhythm disturbance, nightmares, weight gain, water retention, anxiety, and skin irritation (with the patch). After this drug has been used for a while, it must be stopped slowly to prevent sudden blood pressure changes, nervousness, anxiety, irregular pulse, cramps, or sleep disturbance. With care, these potential effects can be avoided.

In general, well-trained physicians are knowledgeable about the actions and interactions of the drugs discussed above. We have discussed some of the more common currently used agents, but in the future, other agents or drugs may also come into use.

4.

OTHER TREATMENTS FOR ADD

Patricia O. Quinn, M.D.

As with any disorder, treatments other than medication have been proposed to address the symptoms of ADD. Over the years, these alternative (and controversial) treatments have included biofeedback, cognitive or self-control therapy, and dietary manipulations. Many of these therapies claim quick and dramatic results. Most have not received extensive scientific study and rely on individual case reports or anecdotal information to support their claims. Although these approaches do not address the neurobiochemical basis of ADD, they do alleviate some of the symptoms and provide additional therapies that may be effective in some cases.

We cannot endorse any of the alternative therapies discussed in this chapter until they can be validated by large, well-controlled group scientific studies. However, after becoming more knowledgeable, you may want to discuss these therapies with your physician or therapist to determine if one may hold particular relevance for you.

Biofeedback and cognitive therapies have recently gained much attention.

BIOFEEDBACK THERAPY

As a standard psychological technique used since the 1960s, biofeedback has been shown to be an effective way of reducing pain, stress, and anxiety. This approach includes deep-breathing exercises and listening to music or guided imagery tapes to achieve relaxation. Research has shown that relaxation or "self-control" training can produce beneficial effects for ADD individuals, but that these effects do not last. A specific form of biofeedback related to teaching a person to relax facial and body muscles, either alone or with muscle tension biofeedback (also called electromyographic biofeedback or EMC), may improve the ability to sit still for longer periods of time, but only while engaged in the therapy. This form of relaxation therapy can also be effective for dealing with sleep disturbances associated with ADD.

In the 1980s, another form of biofeedback therapy emerged specifically for the treatment of ADD. This was promoted by Joel Lubar, a Ph.D. from Knoxville, Tennessee. Dr. Lubar used the sophisticated brain-wave biofeedback training that he had previously used to reduce seizures to reduce the symptoms of ADD. His treatment program is known as EEG biofeedback and is founded on the theory that the brain of the ADD individual is underactive, particularly in the frontal areas (discussed in Chapter 3). Dr. Lubar's treatment is based on the research findings that in people with ADD electrical activity in the frontal areas of the brain is less than in people without ADD. This electrical activity is measured by using an electroencephalogram, or EEG. Improvement of ADD symptoms is the result of training that increases brain-wave activity. The individual is taught to increase brain activity associated with increased attention span and to decrease brain activity associated with daydreaming or distractibility. Dr. Lubar claims dramatic results not only with ADD symptoms but also in increased academic performance and overall cognitive abilities. Unfortunately, there have been few studies using this type of treatment for ADD children, and those that have been done have not been well controlled. While this type of treatment may hold some promise, it needs to be subjected to more rigorous scientific study with replication by others. Meanwhile, such training can be both time-consuming and expensive.

SELF-CONTROL OR COGNITIVE THERAPY

Self-control or cognitive therapy has also been proposed as a means of dealing with some of the symptoms of ADD. It has been shown to improve self-concept and to remediate the lack of self-guiding language-based behaviors seen in ADD individuals. The therapy encompasses both behavior and feelings.

Two of the more important components of self-control therapy are self-instruction and relaxation or calming. Both strategies help with impulsive behaviors, by training the individual to think before acting and to talk to her- or himself about what is happening. The individual is also taught to replace negative self-statements with positive ones, thus improving self-esteem.

Calming therapy is used to deal with the hyperarousal or anger symptoms discussed in Chapter 1. The individual is taught to recognize which situations provoke these symptoms and to talk to him- or herself about what is going on and how he or she is feeling, including physical sensations. Relaxation techniques, including deep breathing and self-talk, are then used to decrease these sensations and feelings. The final step is rewarding yourself with positive statements like "See, that wasn't so bad. I knew I could do it." This kind of self-reinforcement can help in overcoming and coping with negative situations. This program has been shown to be effective, especially when combined with more standard forms of therapy, such as medication and psychotherapy.

DIET AND MEGAVITAMIN THERAPY

Elimination diets and megavitamin therapies have been proven overall to be the least effective of the alternative therapies. Diet therapy as a treatment for ADD became popular over 20 years ago when allergist Dr. Benjamin Feingold proposed the elimination of salicylate-containing foods in children allergic to aspirin. Eventually, dyes and preservatives were also added to the list of offending agents to be eliminated. Although individual cases were found that responded to the elimination of particular agents, no well-controlled scientific study has shown diet to be effective in decreasing hyperactive symptoms for large numbers of people.

Restricted diets can also prove detrimental to overall health.

Other diets have suggested increasing vitamins and minerals. Unfortunately, megavitamin therapy has also proved ineffective as a treatment for ADD. Gaining acclaim in the early 1970s, these treatments quickly proved not only ineffective, but dangerous. Large doses of certain vitamins and minerals can be harmful, and seizures may occur upon rapid withdrawal.

A number of studies have looked at the relationship between excess dietary sugar ingestion and hyperactive behaviors. Most results have been confusing, but a few well-designed studies have shown some effect of sugar on a small number of ADD children. It appears that the timing of rather than the amount of sugar intake is the important factor in influencing symptoms.

The best course for all students, and especially for those with ADD, is a well-balanced, nutritionally sound diet with meals evenly spaced throughout the day. In my practice, I am always amazed by the number of patients who are not eating breakfast or are "skipping meals." For years, nutritional studies have shown these habits to be detrimental to school performance. Errors increase and scores decrease when students are tested in the fasting state. The life-style of the college student does little to reinforce good nutritional habits, but good habits are essential for the ADD individual, who needs extra help to be able to concentrate and carry on effectively and efficiently.

In Chapter 6, college students will further address these issues as they talk about their experiences of living with ADD in high school and college.

5.◆
HOW ADD
AFFECTS YOU

Thomas Applin, M.D.

In the past, parents, teachers, and others assumed that by adolescence, the symptoms of ADD were "outgrown." However, for most people with ADD, certain problems remain in the areas of attention span, impulsiveness, distractibility, and decision making. The claim that one "outgrows" ADHD was based on a decrease in the symptom of hyperactivity alone.

In fact, as teenagers mature, many *do* make improvements in hyperactivity. However, mobilizing attention, mastering the necessary organizational skills, and "reining in" an impulsive learning and behavioral style can be daunting tasks. Academic accommodations, medication, and counseling may still be necessary during the high school and college years.

The majority of young adults recognize that ADD symptoms still pose both academic and social problems. Let's take a look at some of the areas that are particularly important to you, the high school and college student.

This is a difficult time to still be dealing with your ADD

symptoms. The last thing you want is to feel different from your peers. Social life has taken on greater importance. Sports, dating, social activities, and academic demands are all increasing. These changes pose special challenges for everyone, but especially for you who have ADD.

As you mature, identification with peer values and the peer culture increases. Feeling different because of attention-related academic problems or taking medication becomes more and more distasteful. Some deal with the problem by denial. Others recognize but resent both the ADD symptoms and the need to continue to address them. Other emotional reactions to having ADD include "acting out," low self-esteem, and depression.

In addition to dealing with your ADD, you are trying to separate from parents and family and to develop an identity, values, and life of your own. Most teenagers feel the need to break away from parental rules and restrictions. Special education classes, tutoring, and taking stimulant medication for ADHD may be seen as "giving in" to parents or to other authority figures such as doctors or teachers. You may see taking medication as a sign of dependence, weakness, or even defectiveness. This is the opposite of what you are striving for as you move toward independence and a life of decision making without parental involvement.

For some, the rejection of medication and/or other therapies for ADD represents striking a blow for freedom and self-reliance. The desire to be viewed as an individual and not just another statistic is also important. A frequent complaint among young people is, "I'm an individual. Just because other kids my age still need treatment for ADD doesn't mean that I do. I'm doing fine without medication or therapy." This attitude is not a denial of the ADD, but rather reflects a desire to be independent and self-reliant, handling problems alone.

The embarrassment over having to take medication or to leave school on a regular basis for therapy appointments can be a real problem for those with ADD. This point is best illustrated by a patient who told me, "I usually don't need to take the medication, but I do take it to study for tests or on the day of a test." Her embarrassment and denial at times overrode the knowledge that the medication helped her. She would call in times of crisis, and then became tearful when we discussed how her reluctance to take care of her problems with ADD led to these crises.

In addition, during adolescence, social issues are often a dominant concern. Social life and participation in sports can be complicated by ADD and the use of medication. Exposure to drugs and alcohol increases during the high school and college years. The combination of alcohol and other drugs with prescription stimulant medication used to treat ADD can result in dangerous drug interactions. In some cases, adolescents may refuse to take the prescribed medication in order to be able to use recreational drugs, knowing that when recreational and prescription drugs are combined, life-threatening reactions can occur, including cardiac, blood pressure, and respiratory complications. For those who stop their medications, school performance and social interactions can suffer as attentiveness decreases and impulsive behavior increases. Assigned classwork is harder to complete, test performance and grades decrease, and dangerous acting out may result. Stopping medication complicates the problem rather than providing any real solution.

Athletic performance and behavior are other areas directly affected by ADD symptoms. Decreased attention span and distractibility affect sports performance as much as they do a math test. Improved focus and concentration on the game are qualities that may be misinterpreted as decreased aggressive drive, but a cool head on the sports field can be a real asset.

Another common concern of adolescents taking medication for ADD involves the perception of change in personality. Some people with ADD have a tendency to be more active, talkative, and energetic than their peers. When you take stimulant medication, your increased ability to focus, decreased impulsiveness (including talking), and increased ability to reflect before acting can really feel like a dramatic personality change. A 17-year-old girl put it this way: "I'm not as spontaneous, funny, or interesting as I was. My friends tell me I've become too quiet." This feeling of personality change and the sense of being controlled by medication may go against your desire for independence and self-control. However, this may be a choice you wish to make for the benefit of improved performance and achievement. Or, an adjustment in dose of medication by your physician may address some of these concerns.

As adolescence progresses, another task you face involves the ability to exert control over impulses and drives. The impulsiveness of ADD can present an impediment to achieving that control. One student told me of his tendency to become quickly and intensely involved with new friends, extending himself in generous but unrealistic ways. Often, this involvement resulted in an unhappy or even dangerous outcome. Sexual pressures may result in impulsive but unwanted sexual acting out. The impulsiveness of ADD may also lead to delinquent behavior in both boys and girls. Learning to gain control over your drives can be furthered by a number of intervention strategies, including insight, cognitive, and medication therapy.

The increased academic and social demands on older adolescents can be much harder to cope with in an environment that makes fewer accommodations for older students. It is especially important for you to receive both academic and psychological support during the transition into the college environment. The belief that ADD is essentially a disorder of children was at one time fostered by the belief that medication was no longer useful after puberty.

As you have learned from your many experiences with tutoring, psychotherapy, and medication, you *can* improve your attention span, better organize your work, decrease impulsiveness, screen out distractions, and exert control over hyperactivity. However, the support of psychotherapy, medication, and special education may not be as readily available to you as a student of high school or college age. Too often, ADD has been seen as a disorder of childhood only, one that is expected to be self-limiting and eventually outgrown. You need and deserve continued support to help you reach your full potential. Don't let your ADD overcome *you*; get the help you need and learn to manage *it*!

6.

COLLEGE STUDENTS SPEAK ABOUT ADD

The following pages contain personal commentaries from college students who live with ADD. They tell about their experiences and offer suggestions to assist you as you approach your college years.

ERIK

For most graduates, college is remembered as the best years of their lives. For others, college is a long, drawn-out affair that entails many changes, disappointments, and underachievement. I hope that most of you will remember college as a positive experience. During college, you stand to have the best time of your life, but you also have the opportunity to learn and grow as you never have before.

It is a source of great pleasure to see myself change and mature, and notice how much of what I've been taught in class

I've managed to retain and use in my everyday life. Perhaps you've noticed my positive attitude toward college. This is a most important point. It is necessary that you view your education as *your* education. Intrinsic motivation is as vital to a student with ADD as to any other student.

College is full of ups and downs, and, take my word, there *will* be times when you need to motivate from within. But sticking it out and finishing are important.

By many estimates, the majority of new jobs will require a college education. The work force will grow more slowly than at any time since the 1930s. This may force employers to shift to more capital-intensive production systems. This means that manufacturing jobs will continue to be lost to automation, further accelerating the decline of manufacturing in the United States.[1] This is a strong case to stay in school. Your chances of future employment and income level will rise dramatically. Besides, it's fun. Apart from the economics of the job market (if this were an economics class, say microeconomics, you'd have to refer to it as the labor market), other intrinsic middle-class values make college an attractive choice.

When choosing a college, there are several things you owe it to yourself to consider. Your choice of the school you attend will be an important factor in your successful completion. One important issue to consider is the environment in which you will go to school. This obviously includes geographic and meteorological conditions. More important, though, is the academic environment.

At Georgetown University, I am surrounded by an extremely competitive, conservative, motivated, intelligent, and

---

[1] *Workforce 2000*—Copyright 1987 Hudson Institute, Inc. Library of Congress CC# 87-601910.

often annoying and disconcerting student body. As an example, let's look at how this affected me. First of all, it contributed to a sense of intellectual insecurity. Many of the students like to boast of their achievements. I soon learned that I was far from being the most intelligent person around. Not that I was the smartest guy in high school, but I was much closer to the top there. Also, the work was much harder than I had been prepared for in high school. Although this is often the case at college, it was particularly exaggerated at Georgetown. Because my grades were not as high as I had hoped, this contributed to my insecurities.

About this time, I was diagnosed as having ADD, but was not taking Ritalin. My decline continued through the first semester of my sophomore year. At that time, I was reevaluated, and decided to begin taking Ritalin upon the recommendation of a physician.

The change was obvious. Almost immediately, my productivity increased nearly tenfold. My social life, which never had posed any problems, remained much the same. Social interactions seem to be an issue for many ADD individuals, but were not a problem for me.

In looking back, there were a number of other factors contributing to my difficulties. Researchers often state that a stable, structured environment, in conjunction with Ritalin, is the most effective treatment of ADD and ADHD. Nothing could be more true. Students must realize that when they leave home for college, they are also leaving behind the structure and balance that have made treatment most effective. Regular hours are often disrupted by academic strains and the tendency of college students to maintain odd hours. This often entails late nights and early classes. Diet and exercise are also compromised in the transition to college life.

While these conditions influence everybody, they especially affect ADD students. The more sedentary types will notice a dramatic change in overall mental sharpness, and will also feel better with only minimal daily exercise. I do 25 to 50 sit-ups daily, take vitamins, and make a conscious effort to eat a balanced diet. Occasionally I'll swim or lift weights, but not very regularly. The difference is really quite surprising. Try it.

This is a logical point at which to address a related health issue. Ironically, a nation that tells its young to "just say no" to psychotic drugs has become inured to prescribing them. Ritalin (the trade name for methylphenidate hydrochloride) is an amphetamine-type drug, a stimulant. The federal Drug Enforcement Administration (DEA) has classified Ritalin as a Schedule II controlled substance, the most potent category of drugs that can be prescribed. Gene Haisliq, Deputy Assistant Administrator of the DEA Office of Diversion Control, said in an interview, "Its potency ranks right up there with cocaine." Furthermore, Ritalin use has increased enormously in the past few years. In 1988, the number of prescriptions of Ritalin filled and refilled was 14% higher than for the five years before. One percent is a normal growth rate for most prescriptions.[2] Because of growing demand, caused by research indicating that its effects are the same for children, adolescents, and adults, a view that remained in question for many years, the DEA has raised its production ceiling. This has opened debate as to the relationship between the use of psychostimulants on young

---

[2] "Fourth R Is Elementary: Reading, 'Riting, 'Rithmatic–and Ritalin," Fred Boyles and Scott McCarthy. *Los Angeles Herald-Examiner,* April 5, 1988.

people and the increased probability of drug abuse later in life. The long-term research clearly indicates that there is no documented increase in drug abuse in later life if psychostimulants are taken during childhood or adolescence. Other studies have raised concern about drug abuse in later life, particularly considering the evidence that a familial tendency toward alcoholism is seen in families with hyperactive children.

The warning label on your prescription should be heeded. Stimulants should not be used with alcohol or other drugs. In college, drugs are far more prevalent than in high school. In addition to interactions with Ritalin (especially with cocaine; the combination of the two stimulants can easily cause respiratory failure and it increases the probability of an overdose), drugs also pose a number of other problems. First, drugs will upset the balance you have achieved. Second, they will work to destroy your motivation and health. Third, the implications of addiction, outside the obvious physical ones, are very serious—expulsion from school, jail, or death. They pose a big risk to your chances for the future success that you as individuals with ADD or ADHD have worked harder than most to attain. Stay away.

Finally, as stated earlier, a positive self-image, environmental factors, and mental and physical fitness are the primary issues to be concerned with during college, particularly if you have ADD. In a certain sense, college is a zen experience. Great strides can be made. One must be ever watching the mind and body. It's very personal. Become conscious of who you are, where you're going, how you're growing, and what you're doing. The idea is mental freedom and transformation of the familiar. Stay busy, in phase, and in love. Carpe diem.

CHRIS

My name is Chris Willingham. I am a 19-year-old sophomore at Davidson, which is right outside Charlotte, North Carolina. I graduated from a high school in Bethesda, Maryland, in 1991. I was fortunate to be diagnosed as having attention deficit disorder early—in second grade—when my teachers began to realize that I was having problems. I was zoning out in class. I met with a developmental pediatrician and she started me on Ritalin. I was able to get control of my school work very early on in high school. As an ADD student, you can do a lot. It's certainly not something that needs to hold you back. I was class president during my sophomore, junior, and senior years; I played football for four years; I ran track; and I became an Eagle Scout. I started a community service program at my school that benefited the elderly, and I was on the honor roll for the last three years every quarter. I'm very proud I was able to do all those things even though I did have ADD.

For the most part, my high school offered many favorable conditions for a student with ADD. The counselors were understanding, knowledgeable, and cooperative. Most teachers followed the recommendations of my counselors, my pediatrician, my parents, and myself. However, I cannot claim to have avoided the resistance of some teachers. A few were not very willing to assist me. This resistance from teachers stemmed from one thing, basically, their ignorance of attention deficit disorder. They were either misinformed on the subject, dismissed the experts' claims, or were completely ignorant about its existence. I was passed off by many as not being a hard worker, less driven than other students, and, as quite simply put by a few of my teachers, lazy. It always frustrated me because they didn't seem to understand how hard I actually had to work to accomplish the same things that the student next to me did, and that it took a lot more willpower and inner drive for me to do that than they could ever understand. It was very frustrating. It was hard for me to communicate that to them.

Many didn't believe that the diagnosis of ADD was valid because the symptoms are common among many students. Everyone zones out in class every once in a while. Everyone reads a page and says, "What did I just read?" And everyone can come to a problem on a test and have to skip it. But for a student with ADD, these problems are magnified. I would read an entire chapter and wonder, "What did I just read?" I would zone out constantly in class, and then I'd get called on and have to realize where I was. And when I got stuck on a problem, I could skip that problem, but then I'd get stuck with the next one; I'd skip that problem, and get stuck with the next one. It's a lot worse for a student with ADD.

Other teachers doubted my need for special help because the symptoms weren't apparent in common conversation. Some teachers, when I'd tell them I had attention deficit disorder, would say, "Oh. Oh, OK–I can help you." They would speak loudly and slowly. I never said I was deaf, but there's such a vast misunderstanding. Others just immediately assumed that I was going to abuse my special circumstances. I had to earn the trust of all my teachers, and that was very, very, difficult. I did it, and you can do it as well simply by never cheating. I never cheated– well, I cheated on one test in high school and I felt so guilty that I turned myself in. I got a "D," but I do think the teacher respected me. I never plagiarized a paper, and after a while, my teachers started to realize that I was honest. I earned their trust. When I needed extra time on a test, the teacher would say, "OK, Chris, I trust you. Here, you just sit down here in this room by yourself and take it." My books could be in the room with me and there was never any problem.

The abuse of, or the suspicion of abusing, your circumstances is also something that is very easily recognized by your peers, or at least by my peers. I tried to keep it as secret as I could that I had ADD, but when everyone else has to turn in their test papers and I'm still working, and they come back an hour later and I'm still there, it looks very suspicious. My friends would say, "Oh, if I had extra time, too, sure, I'd be able to do this." It was hard for me to convince them that I would rather be in their shoes, I'd much rather not have ADD and not need help than have ADD and need help. Because even if you have unlimited time on a test, after a while your brain just starts to go. If you have been sitting down and working on a test for three hours, believe me, the last thing you want to do is check your problems over and check everything a second time. You just want to get out of there. There were many times I would be taking a test and I knew I needed to spend more time to do well, but I just needed to get outside. I needed a breath of fresh air. There are different ways to deal with this, and I'll discuss them later.

The first problem in high school, then, is encountering resistance from your peers and teachers, but if you establish trust and respect, you can go far, very far.

As a student with ADD, I encountered academic problems. These included memorization of facts, problem solving, and reading comprehension. To aid in memorization of facts, I'd use different cue terms and poems and acronyms. I was careful to study definitions both ways because they could be presented either way on the test. I did not just use mental images, but knew the facts.

Logic and problem solving were not difficult for me. I think I could figure things out better than most people. It just took me a lot more time to do it. I needed to concentrate, and to keep down the mental fatigue as well.

Reading comprehension was much more of a problem. I would miss key terms or read over them in a paragraph. A paragraph could be in a completely different tense or totally different gender and I wouldn't even realize it. I would miss one word and need to keep going back and reading the passage over again and again. I'd read it and it didn't make any sense. This was because I had missed the one word. You have to be really careful when you're reading, or at least I did, so you don't miss anything.

Another problem I had with reading comprehension was my actual attention to the facts. If I wanted to retain all the facts in a given passage, I had to read them very slowly and almost examine every word, or else I would lose them. This can be a special problem with SATs and other standardized tests. There's usually a reading comprehension section on which they ask you questions afterward, and you have to be able to answer them. I usually had to read over these passages at least three times before I could answer the questions.

Besides reading comprehension, reading anything was really a chore just because of the amount of time it took. It takes me about five minutes to read a page in a novel. It can take me up to 15 minutes to read one page in a textbook. This is just an enormous amount of time—time I didn't have.

Here are the methods I came up with to help. If you're

reading a novel, first read the Cliff notes or some summary (I'm not saying you should *just* read the Cliff notes). You read the Cliff notes first so you have a basic idea of what is going on. Then if you miss a key word or key term, it doesn't throw you off. It is also important to discuss your reading with a friend afterward. You may be looking at it from one perspective and he may be coming at it from another; if you share those perspectives, you'll gain a much better picture of the whole concept. It's very rare that you're going to miss something entirely and he's going to miss it, too.

The same is true when reading textbooks. It's really helpful when there's a chapter summary before the chapter. It's also important always to read the bold print. If you read through all the bold print, all the highlighted information and outlines, then you'll understand what is going on. In addition, read any questions in the back of the book or chapter first, then read just to answer these questions. This will give you a good idea of the basic points. You can then skim through and you will have all the facts that you're going to need.

And above all else, in everything you do, whenever you have a problem, talk to your teacher or professor. They enjoy teaching and like to talk to the students. This is especially true at the college level. Many college students feel intimidated about going to their professors' offices, or going to dinner or lunch with them. They really want you to learn, and they can help you a lot. If you talk to your professors, you're going to do so much better. I wish more college students realized that.

Other accommodations are also useful. The main accommodation I had to receive was extra time on tests. This, however, is *not* the *only* solution; even though you have extra time, you still need to know all the material. Otherwise you're going to be guessing. If you need to guess most of the time, you're going to find that your test takes hours and your brain is going to go to jelly. Basically, finish as quickly as possible so that you can avoid this mental fatigue. If you need to take a break, take a break. If you have to go to the bathroom, go to the bathroom. If you're hungry, get something to eat. If you're thirsty, go get a drink. You want to make it as comfortable for yourself as possible. If you have to go the bathroom during a test and just sit there, you're not going to do as well. This may seem simple, but it is true, especially for someone with ADD. If you have something else on your mind, you're not going to do as well. You want to remove any unnecessary distractions.

SATs, I would say, were my biggest challenge. I took untimed SATs and I did very well. I got a 1480, but it took me *eight hours*! I mean I was the only person there. This lady was so mad at me because I was making her stay there on Saturday. She checked her watch, I swear, every 30 seconds. Eight hours it took me, but I'm glad I stuck in there and took the extra time because it really helped me. When taking untimed SATs, they are very generous about letting you eat, take breaks, and get drinks. You have to make sure that you have enough rest and a full stomach.

Well, that's how I got through high school. Now I would like to talk briefly about college. For me, the workload was overwhelming.

I decided to be a political science major, which requires a great deal of reading, but I'm doing what I want to do. I'm enjoying it, and I think that is really important. If you're going to do well, you have to enjoy what you're doing. If you don't enjoy it, you are going to lose your attention quickly—that's a problem I have always had.

it, you are going to lose your attention quickly—that's a problem I have always had.

I'd also like to say something on behalf of small schools. There's more of a community atmosphere, and people and professors really want to help you. This may be true of large schools as well, but I am speaking from my experience. Large schools may also have much larger facilities and resources to help you, but at a small school, there is a lot of personal attention for someone with a learning disability.

Very briefly, I also want to relate my experience with Ritalin. It really helped me. I would probably describe it as a wonder drug. It's not a wonder drug for everyone who takes it, but it was for me. I take two 20 mg sustained-release tablets daily. I started Ritalin in my sophomore year of high school and I maintained a steady 3.76 GPA, so something happened. I think it was the Ritalin; it helped me a lot. I do have side effects though. I find that I have to take it on a full stomach or else I have stomachaches. I also find that when I take it all year long and come off it for the summer, I have minimal withdrawal headaches and some stomachaches, which last about two or three days. I experience nothing that would keep me from participating fully in life's activities, and I think it did a lot of good for me. Whether it will for you, I don't know, but I hope so. I also hope that you all can be successful and enjoy yourselves as much as possible even though you have attention deficit disorder.

7.

PREPARING FOR COLLEGE: A Mother's Perspective

Elayne Clift, M.A.

Some kids take to college like fish to water. Our daughter thought she would be one of them. She had graduated in the top 10% of a nationally recognized high school. She was popular and success-ful, taking leading roles in the school plays and serving as editor of the literary magazine. Her SATs were respectable, her rec-ommendations stellar. She couldn't get there fast enough.

After a day of parent orientation during which we fell in love with the small liberal arts college she had chosen, we dropped her off at the dorm, a "happy camper" ready for the big adven-ture. It was all downhill from there. The phone calls started the next day. "I don't think I can stay here," she whispered. "I hate it and I feel awful. I don't really like the people here. I'm not going to fit in."

During the week of orientation for "first years," her sense of being alone and different centered around her discomfort socially. We tried to assure her that these things take time and that it was much too early to judge. Because she is not "a party animal" and does not drink, she felt out of sync with campus life. We explained that for many kids, heavy partying and drinking were a way of denying their own anxiety. Such interpretation and advice made sense in her mind, but did little to help her feel better.

Predictably, the week that classes began, she grew more depressed and anxious. Her phone calls became more frequent and more frantic. She confessed that she felt scared, inadequate, and overwhelmed. I knew she was unhappy and that her feelings were beginning to interfere with her getting things done. Everything seemed too much to handle. Consequently, she was having difficulty keeping up with her school work, feeling unable even to write the first paper. Her dad and I spent long hours on the phone counseling, encouraging, trying to keep it in perspective for her. We encouraged her to call whenever she wanted. Her father got a copy of *Bleak House* and read it furiously so that he could stimulate ideas for her paper. We worried about her, and hoped that it would, as we told her, get better.

By the end of the first week, I decided a visit from me would be a good idea. She had managed to keep putting one foot in front of the other, to get to class, to do a little work, and to make some friends. She had also instinctively and with great maturity taken the right steps toward coping. She was seeing a counselor, had discussed her anxiety with her English teacher and been given an extension on the paper, and had shared her feelings with a few friends while keeping up a brave and cheerful front. Still, I felt my daughter needed a mom, and a jumpstart with some of the practical things that were overwhelming her. When I first suggested I visit, she said No. It would be embarrassing, she explained, for her friends to think she "needed Mommy." And she wanted desperately to do it on her own.

"Fine. Let's see how it goes then," we agreed.

Three hours later, she was on the phone asking me to come.

During the week that I was there, we spent a good deal of time exploring in wonderful conversations what was happening. In spite of her sense that she just wasn't "getting any of it," I saw remarkable growth. I found my daughter not only more mature, but more likeable than when she had left home only two short weeks before. I wished that she could believe me when I told her that, and that it really would be all right because she had what it takes to succeed as a student, and as a human being. She knew that I spoke from experience and that she could trust what I was telling her. She just couldn't quite believe it. We cried together, and we laughed at how crazy we must have looked crying. We both tried to know that it would be okay.

We also spent time on a number of practical issues. We did the laundry, balanced her checkbook, visited the study skills center, and worked on a time management calendar. We went to see her faculty advisor and her counselor. We took care of her holiday travel home and her bookstore and clothing needs—in short, those aspects of life that just seemed too much. We spent time apart, each doing our work, and reconvened when it was time to work something out or talk some more. We each went to bed at night exhausted, physically and emotionally, but with a few more milestones achieved. I'm sure my being there was the right thing, in spite of some campus "experts" who made me feel like a meddling mom.

At the end of the week, things weren't a whole lot better, but we had struck a deal. She would hang on till fall break—a long weekend opportunity to be at home—and then we would discuss whether a transfer, or a year out, would be appropriate. If she continued to feel very uncomfortable with the school atmosphere, we would support her decision to make a change. The important thing for her to know was that there were other options, that she was not trapped. We just wanted whatever happened to be a sound decision and not a defeat. As parents, we walked the fine line between firm and fair. And we ached for her pain.

By the time the long October weekend rolled around, the phone calls had become somewhat less frequent. That first awesome paper was complete and early grades were more than encouraging. She had, with much encouragement, auditioned for and "made" choir, and she had been to several social functions. While she was still not happy, her mood was decidedly improved, and she was coping in measurably better ways. She was even able, occasionally, to laugh at some of the things that irritated her. Our daughter, we reflected, was growing up.

As it happened, the conversation we had been so careful to plan when she came home was far less agonized than we all had anticipated. In her own time, and in her own way, our daughter had come to realize that sticking it out for a year was the sensible thing to do. "I want this to work," she said thoughtfully. "They say things get better after first semester. And in a lot of ways, it is a good school for me. If only I can find a group of kids I feel comfortable with, maybe it will be okay. If not, we'll see." Her conclusions after the first six weeks, simply put, mirrored our own.

A week later, we were on campus for Parents' Weekend. "You have a fine daughter," one of her professors told us. "I know she is having a hard time and I can understand why. I have some of the same problems myself, as a newcomer here. But she is a special kind of student, thoughtful and mature. I think she'll be okay."

We thought so too as teary-eyed we said our farewells until Thanksgiving, and watched our "first year" stride, pensive but purposeful, into the noisy solitude of the dormitory.

My daughter, who is a sophomore as I write this and who still has some bad days, was recently diagnosed as having attention deficit disorder. I think what happened to her is so typical of most kids' experience when they go away to school that I asked her permission to share her story.

Leaving home is never easy. Learning how "to do" college, or be on your own, is not easy either. Almost all kids have adjustment problems of one kind or another. For kids with learning disabilities (like my son) or ADD (like my daughter), it can feel even more troubling, especially if you think you are the only one going through tough times.

Here are some things that I think can help. Talk them over with your friends and your folks. And remember, if the going gets tough, you're not alone! There's help on campus, and off. Just remember, a lot of us have been through it, and most of us make it, really.

Trust me. I'm a mom!

HELPFUL HINTS

♦ Learn some of the practical lessons of life before you go away so that doing laundry, balancing a checkbook, and managing time don't seem overwhelming in addition to the academic pressure. Do as much hands-on learning as it takes for these tasks to seem like second nature. Responsibilities at home can also help to build a sense of competence and to introduce you to the idea of time management.

♦ Trust your own sense, and your parents', about what you need in order to feel supported. Leaving home and dealing with identity, intimacy, independence, and academic and social life are major life adjustments. College counselors and others like to think that a student must find his or her own way. Psychologists are trained to believe that adolescence is the time to do this, even if it is difficult. Often, without meaning to, they convey the feeling that your parents' interventions are inappropriate. If professional advice doesn't feel right to you (like telling you that you have to "do it" on your own), follow your own best instincts. You and your folks know best what your strengths and weaknesses are. (At the same time, your parents need to respect the choices you make. You might really rather be a dancer than a doctor!)

♦ Understand that your adjustment experience is not unique. It may seem like all the other kids are doing just fine, but a good percentage of them are not. "War stories" abound about the emotional upsets that people have experienced when they go to school. The vast majority of them survive!

♦ Keep things in perspective. The adjustment is a life crisis, but it is not a catastrophe and you are not trapped. Options exist and can be explored at the right time. Some students elect to drop out for a semester to get their footing and then return. Others realize that campus life is not for them and go on to be day students elsewhere. Some conclude that they need a year to mature before they can handle the academic pressure. There are no real mistakes, only lessons. The process of learning takes time. Try to keep a sense of proportion, and a sense of humor.

♦ Find out what support services exist on campus and use them. Virtually all schools offer academic tutoring, writing centers, counseling services, peer counseling, resident advisors in the dorms, and so on. Seek such help. It is the strong adult who knows when and where to ask for help, not the weak child.

♦ Give yourself permission to feel sad and don't expect too much of yourself. Sooner or later, the cloud will lift.

♦ If feelings of discomfort persist, there is probably a valid reason. You may feel "out of sync" with the school you have chosen and its values. Such insight is a sign of maturity and should be affirmed. It is not defeat to leave as long as you have given it a fair chance. Most people agree that means at least a semester, if not a full year.

AND WHAT ABOUT THE FOLKS?

What will it be like for them when you have gone? Here are just a few of the things we parents feel:

Curious

What will it really be like for you, and how will you change as time goes on? How will the family change without you? Parents can't predict what the changes will be, but they know, partly because of the slight uneasiness they feel with you gone, that things won't be the same once the kids have grown up and started to make their own way.

Worried

Will you be all right? Despite every confidence in the world about how capable you are, you are still their little boy or girl. It's hard not to be there to make the boo-boos feel better.

Sad

It isn't just full-time moms who experience the "empty nest syndrome." Even workaholic parents feel very sad at the "loss" when one of their favorite people goes away. Separation anxiety isn't only for kids.

Relieved

Things have probably been pretty uptight during the senior year at high school, and in a way, it feels good to be free of the tension. Moms and dads look forward to some quiet time together, doing some of the things they never had time for when you were small.

Supportive

Parents still want to be needed. And they DO remember what it's like to be away from home and to wrestle with all the stresses of school life. Their own coping skills are somehow strengthened as they watch you grow, and they are eager to share what they know about surviving life.

Proud

Your folks know what a tough job leaving home is. Learning to manage everything from laundry to checkbooks, from studies to new friends and intimate relationships, is a life adjustment they've made—and survived—too. They know you have the intelligence to make good decisions and the ability to succeed. They take pleasure in your accomplishments, and when you're happy, they're happy for you.

So remember, the phone and the mail work both ways. Every once in a while, just check in with the folks to see how they're doing with it all. They could use the support, even if they do sound like they're just fine!

8.

WHAT TO EXPECT DURING HIGH SCHOOL SENIOR YEAR

Elayne Clift, M.A.

SEPTEMBER

The mailbox suddenly bursts with assorted catalogues and recruitment propaganda. Fathers are seen to wander around muttering about the state of the family's savings. You alternate between "The Grinch Who Stole Summer" and the "sweetest thing who ever lived." The college quest has begun. Unofficially, the rite of passage began some time earlier, with PSATs and preliminary meetings with the guidance counselor. But this is serious.

OCTOBER

You take the SATs and compete with your friends on the phone about who did worse. Your guidance counselor holds a meeting

Editor's note: Some of these things may happen even before senior year. _POQ_

for parents about the process over the coming year, and what
to expect of the kids. They will run the gamut, parents are told,
between sulky and surly. A parent's job is to be supportive. (This
is not easy when your son or daughter continually sounds like
"The Little Engine Who Couldn't": "I won't get in! I won't get
in!") College visits, which may have started in the spring or
summer, take place. These are actually opportunities to enjoy
and get to know your parents better. In the sanctity of an
airplane or a car, things seem easier to say. It's okay to confess
being scared, or excited, or nervous.

NOVEMBER

Applications start rolling in. It is time to complete those for
which early decision is sought. You have mood swings ranging
from frolicking to furious, dedicated to despairing, adorable to
obnoxious. You may say things like this to your parents: "I'm
supposed to get angry with you so that I can leave!" They
understand. By the end of the month, everyone is on pins and
needles waiting for SAT scores and early admission.

DECEMBER

The scores come back, and so do the first rejections. Your
counselor reminds you that her door is always open. In reality,
it is not; there is already another senior (or her mother) in
there, probably clutching a box of tissues. Seniors who have not
been lucky enough to receive an early acceptance, and those
who have not are the majority, may feel despondent. Christmas

doesn't seem as much fun. Chocolate chip cookies and presents under the tree help. Parents grow weary. A certain amount of vacation time may be devoted to filling out more applications. Happily, many schools now accept the common application, which is enough in itself to put a school on the "short list." The required essays seem odious, but they always get done. Deadlines loom, but they always get met. Parents "just don't understand," but they help out anyway.

JANUARY

The calm before the storm. Applications are in, last exams are over, there's nothing more to be done but wait. You suddenly seem very mature to your parents.

FEBRUARY

Like January, but colder.

MARCH

The month starts quietly, but tension quickly mounts. By mid-month, the only way to get a call in or out of your house is to declare an emergency. If it's not you and your friends comparing mail, it's parents confessing that the empty nest syndrome has hit in a big way. Parents spend a good part of evenings and weekends reading the latest literature on "How to Finance a College Education." Tattered references like "The Complete

Guide to Colleges and Universities" are only consulted now if an acceptance comes in. By the end of the month, victories are being celebrated, wounds licked, choices made. You are relieved. And happy for each other. You are also beginning to realize that, pretty soon, high school really will be over. It will be time to part from old friends, family, familiar routines. It is scary and exciting, and most of the time, you are able to tell which is which. The nice thing is, you've started sharing some of this with the folks in an adult and interesting manner. You begin actually to like each other.

APRIL

More visits. This time it is serious. A school will be chosen. It needs to feel right. Sometimes that visceral reaction will come from the weather, the tour guide, the cafeteria, the library, the admissions office waiting room. But as sure as ivy grows on walls, it will come. You just know when the place is right for you. By the end of the month, like a long and arduous task, it is over. And that is when it really begins.

MAY

In the flurry of final school activities, all is excitement, anticipation, the sweet smell of success. Your parents are curiously more somber. But among your friends, everyone is happy, relieved, congratulatory.

JUNE

Prom night excitement gives way to the thrill and emotion of graduation. Parents and kids alike weep to "Pomp and Circumstance," just as they have always done. Kids party, parents party, and sometimes, they even party together. Parents know that their children are on the way to being responsible adults. They feel glad, sad, and something else, in their stomachs and throats, that they just can't seem to put their fingers on.

JULY

You and your parents scour the catalogues and discount stores for bargains on sheets, towels, sweats, lamps, boom boxes, computers, and other necessities of college life. Foot lockers and trunks begin to be loaded and labeled. Good-byes begin to be said as classmates leave for vacations and jobs.

AUGUST

Your parents, if they are lucky, take a couple of weeks off to recover. (You probably refuse to go with them.) At the end of the month, station wagons are loaded, final farewells are said, last bits of advice are shared, tears are shed. Your mom says "Clean up your room!" for the last time. "Don't forget to call," she mandates and Dad repeats. "I'm really going to miss you," is whispered in private, low, slightly shaky voices.

It is time to leave. It is hard. You tell yourselves, and each other, that it will be okay. It will. Parents have done the best they can, and you know it. You have what it takes, and your parents know it. Come to think of it, they always did. And so did you. It just took the college countdown to prove it.

9.

LOOKING AT COLLEGE PROGRAMS

Kathleen O'Connor, Ph.D.

Students with ADD and their parents are usually quite focused on ADD-related problems as they begin looking at colleges. They are often unpleasantly surprised to find that most colleges have few resources in place to help students with ADD, and some are unaware that such a condition even exists. Colleges are concerned with campus security, budget cuts, and producing a winning basketball team, but there is little interest in attention deficit disorder. The simple truth is that ADD is not a very squeaky wheel; consequently, it gets very little oil.

This is not to suggest that you should throw your hands up in resignation. Help is available; it will just take a little extra work to find it. Keep in mind that the important thing is to find a college where you, as an individual, with your strengths and weaknesses, will thrive, succeed, and graduate. It is of absolutely no value to gain admission to a competitive, prestigious school and drop out after two semesters. In other words, be realistic.

The first question usually is, "Where do I begin?" Some schools have a comprehensive learning-disabled program and describe it in depth in their catalogue. Some offer nothing. Still others actually offer programs that will help students with ADD, but do not list them as such. Unfortunately, as any consumer knows, what it says on the label is not always what you get in the package. However, the label does provide clues.

Many colleges and universities have offices called Office of Special Services or Office of Student Disability Services or Learning Support Services. In such offices, you can find people whose primary function is to help and advise students with an array of disabilities. If there are people on campus able to help students with ADD, this is the first place to try to find them. Some schools have a program in place specifically designed to address the needs of students with ADD. Other schools may tell you that they have never heard of ADD. Do not despair! Programs designed for students with other disabilities can often be quite effective for students with attention deficits.

What is important is to understand fully the nature and extent of your own particular disability, and to make sure that the college administrators you are dealing with also have a clear picture. To ensure this, bring all documentation relevant to your condition, including any testing, diagnoses, or evaluations by school officials, psychologists, and physicians. Plus, make a written list of the specific support services you believe you need. For example, many students request a reduced course load. If you wish to do this, make sure you tell the college officials about your academic difficulties. Never assume they just know. In most cases, they don't.

Support services that students with ADD may find helpful are priority scheduling, a reduced course load, exam accommodations, single dorm rooms, note takers, editors, tutors, special orientation, counselors, and faculty advocates. Let's take a look at these services and see if some of them might help you.

PRIORITY SCHEDULING

While most college students can cope quite well with a wide range of courses spread throughout the day, the student with ADD often cannot. You will likely do better if classes are scheduled very carefully, considering the time of day, the length of the class, and the professor. Obtaining permission to select your classes before the entire student body registers enhances your chances of controlling your schedule.

REDUCED COURSE LOAD

It is also important that you not become overwhelmed. One way to avoid this is to take a lighter course load, thus enabling you to spend more time on fewer courses.

SPECIAL TEST AREAS

You may find that you are often distracted in large rooms with many other students. This causes you to lose concentration while taking examinations, and thus to score lower than students without disabilities of similar aptitude and ability. If you are allowed to take exams in small, quiet rooms with few distractions, you are more likely to achieve higher test scores.

SINGLE DORM ROOM

Again, the advantage here is that in a single dorm room, you will face fewer distractions than if you had a roommate. It's tough enough living with your own mess and clutter; it's doubly difficult when someone else's is added.

NOTE TAKERS, EDITORS, AND TUTORS

Some students with ADD have difficulty taking notes in class. Thus, when it comes time for review and study, you are at a terrific disadvantage. Note takers can help in class, while editors and tutors can assist you with assignments and papers, and offer supplementary instruction or reinforcement of subject matter.

SPECIAL ORIENTATION

Developed specifically for students with disabilities, these programs offer opportunities for new students to get to know classmates who also need special services. You are introduced to campus life and presented with an overview of available resources. In addition, advice on scheduling may be provided during these sessions.

COUNSELORS

Almost every college or university has a counseling center. Counselors, therapists, and psychologists can help the student recognize the strains created by ADD, and work out ways of coping. Additional diagnostic testing may also be available through these centers.

ADVOCATES

Teachers are often unaware that a student suffers from ADD, and instead may attribute poor academic performance to a lack of effort. Try to find someone on campus who knows the faculty and has a good rapport with them. Nurture a relationship with that person and explain your problem. Ask to be introduced to faculty members. Some teachers may be very sympathetic and helpful; some may not. It is essential that you find an advocate who understands your difficulties and can help you communicate your needs to your professors.

WHEN CHOOSING
A COLLEGE

There are basically five different categories of colleges to consider. You need to choose the type of program that meets your needs. The categories are as follows:

Colleges with Comprehensive Support Programs

These are institutions that offer:

♦ Long-standing support programs dedicated to helping students who have special needs.

♦ A full-time professional staff of trained specialists who play an active role in the admissions process

♦ Special classes, such as: Developmental Math and English, Time Management, and Study Skills

♦ A full menu of support services, such as: special orientation programs, tutors, computers, note takers, scribes, untimed testing, and counselors

Colleges with Limited Support Services

These are characterized by:

♦ A limited version of a comprehensive program

♦ Specialists, whose work usually begins only after the student is admitted

♦ Few, if any, developmental classes

♦ Limited accommodations such as untimed testing and tutors

Colleges with Developmental Programs

These schools:

♦ Combine the underachiever, learning disabled, and students with ADD

◆ Offer special classes such as Developmental Math and English, Time Management, and Study Skills

◆ Have a restricted curriculum for one or two years

◆ Require strict academic monitoring

Colleges Specializing in Students with Learning Disabilities

Currently there are only two of these institutions in the United States–Beacon College in Florida and Landmark College in Vermont. Their sole mission is to provide higher education to students with learning problems. Though not geared specifically toward students with ADD, the programs would no doubt be helpful to them.

Colleges That Are Totally Oblivious to ADD

Unfortunately, many institutions fall into this category. As much as you might want to, don't try to enlighten them. Focus your efforts on the colleges that have shown a willingness to reach out to those with learning problems.

Sometimes, parents and students feel overwhelmed by the obstacles before them. They often ask, "Is college worth it?" The answer is a resounding "YES!" Studies have shown that those who persist and earn a college degree find more satisfying jobs, make more money, and have higher self-esteem than those who do not finish college. So, whatever you do, don't give up!

10.
LEARNING ACCOMMODATIONS FOR ADD STUDENTS

Anne McCormick, M.Ed.
in collaboration with Faith Leonard, Ph.D.

Learning accommodations for individuals with ADD at the college level are as unique as the types and severity of ADD symptoms themselves. Nevertheless, there are two keys to being sure that the necessary adaptations for *your* learning style are provided at the college of your choice. First, the college learning center should be a well established one, with a history of serving students with learning disabilities. This strong foundation should indicate that wisdom of experience prevails and that unique learning accommodations will be welcomed with assurance and understanding. The program's longevity may also ensure that the staff is properly trained in the field of special education.

As college programs for students with learning disabilities have grown, a shortage of well-trained and experienced learning specialists has developed. Students with ADD should be able to feel confident that basic accommodations, such as untimed testing, can be provided for them. Indeed, when the mechanisms for providing adaptations are securely in place and the learning specialists are experienced, the process for obtaining accommodations is not only simplified, but assured.

The other key to guaranteeing individualized accommodations is the student's self-knowledge and acceptance of the ADD. The first step to advocacy is a thorough understanding of how your disability affects your ability to demonstrate intellectual capability, which can be masked by the many symptoms of ADD. In turn, this can create inaccurate measures of your actual ability.

The emotional overlay of a disability and a lack of self-knowledge is frequently more difficult to surmount than the hierarchical ladder you may need to negotiate to secure accommodations. All too often, students with learning disabilities and ADD come to college with the idea of beginning with a "clean slate." In fact, it is still common for students with these disabilities to have received information assuring them and their families that they will outgrow the learning disability or ADD. Therefore, they see college as a chance to start anew without the traditional supports (tutoring, even medication) that some have had for 10 or more years. Though the emotional high of starting college may mask low self-esteem issues, years of repeated frustrations, both personal and academic, make individuals with ADD incredibly vulnerable to the social and academic struggles that lie ahead. This fragile emotional profile leaves students prone to a crisis surrounding accommodations that some do not even want to admit are needed. Staff who coordinate specialized testing programs for learning-disabled students are often faced with students' last-minute acceptance of the need for learning accommodations. In order to secure proper space and proctoring for specialized testing, advance notice to the professor and learning center staff is necessary. Students who belatedly decide that they need help create their own crises by arriving unannounced to take an untimed test. It is difficult to provide the accommodations without prior notice that would allow the student to perform at his or her level of competence.

You can be your own best advocate by knowing who you are and what learning accommodations will assist you in revealing your capabilities, both personal and academic. While an individual with ADD may be well prepared for college, he or she may not have the expertise needed to design accommodations that will highlight his or her capabilities. The Center for Psychological and Learning Services at The American University has compiled a list of common learning problems students at the college level may have. They are categorized into academic and emotional difficulties. No student will exhibit all of the characteristics listed here. The degree to which these characteristics are manifest will also vary greatly depending on each individual's profile of strengths and weaknesses.

ACADEMIC DIFFICULTIES

♦ Organization of time and place is a major problem for many students at the college level and beyond. Frequently, it is the very freedom from structured time craved by the student that becomes a nemesis. People with ADD can become so consumed by the complexity of getting everything done that they do nothing.

♦ Reading problems for persons with ADD frequently center around difficulty in persevering with the task over a length of time. Frequently, when tested for reading problems, these students do much better when time constraints are lifted. In addition, students with ADD may not be able to remember what they read because of attention deficits.

♦ Mathematics is an area of concern for students with ADD, again because of attention problems. Problem solving requires close attention and time. The longer the task takes, the more difficult the task can become. In addition, as time passes and anxiety mounts, visual distortions or reversals can sabotage even basic calculations.

♦ Note taking may be an impossible task for some students with ADD because two skills are called upon simultaneously, listening and writing. In addition, retaining information, even momentarily, can be very difficult, thus causing frustration, which then increases anxiety and interferes with processing information. Also, students with ADD can be so intent on getting everything down that, in the end, it is difficult to organize or even make sense of the notes taken.

♦ Writing for students with ADD can be difficult from two perspectives: it requires both sustained attention and organizational skills, which are frequently the areas affected by their disability.

♦ Verbal skills can be subject to word choice or word retrieval problems as the language skills for conversation or presentation are compromised by the concomitant anxiety of an attention deficit disorder.

♦ Foreign language studies can also be difficult for some who have language or auditory processing problems.

EMOTIONAL DIFFICULTIES

♦ An uneasy relationship with the disability can sabotage the process of securing accommodations.

♦ High levels of frustration are easily triggered by anxiety.

♦ Inappropriate social skills or impulsivity and manipulation can affect interactions with professors and others.

♦ Confusion about goals and the future can hinder attempts to persevere with academic challenges.

All students wrestle with academic and emotional struggles in college but for students with ADD the problems are often more severe and longer lasting. However, with determination and accommodations, students with disabilities can succeed at the college level. You can start by consulting with professors at the beginning of the semester regarding the types of modifications that you may require, given that ADD affects every student differently and to a different degree. Although special modifications in classroom procedures may be needed, academic standards remain the same. Academic ability is not the issue; it is the methods of meeting academic standards that may differ from those of other students.

COMMON ACCOMMODATIONS

Lecture Classes

During lecture classes, the ADD student may:

◆ need to copy the notes of another student in class and may ask the professor's assistance in finding a note taker

◆ need to sit in the front of the room

◆ benefit from the use of visual aids, handouts, and the blackboard

◆ need to use a laptop computer

Writing Papers

When writing papers, ADD students may:

◆ need to meet with professors for clarification of writing assignments

◆ wish to have rough drafts evaluated

◆ require extra time to complete writing assignments

◆ use an editor for papers before submitting final drafts

Examinations

During exams, ADD students may:

◆ need extended time to complete exams and/or administration in an environment free of distraction

♦ need to alter the response format of a test

♦ need to take exams over a period of time in short intervals

Auxiliary Aids

ADD students may also:

♦ need to record lectures

♦ need to use a calculator

♦ need to use a computer for writing assignments

♦ need to order textbooks on tape from the Recordings for the Blind (a process that requires getting a book list well in advance of the course)

OTHER ACCOMMODATIONS

We have also compiled a few (nonstandard) adaptions that students have designed to accommodate their unique learning styles.

Lecture Classes

ADD students may need to arrange with the professor to sit by the door so that after a half an hour he or she can quietly leave and walk around for two or three minutes.

Writing

The ADD student may find it helpful to write and pass in papers in stages.

Examinations

ADD students may do better on take home exams or if they record exams and pass the tape in as a final copy.

Reading

ADD students may find it helpful to break the reading into manageable chunks over a number of reading sessions. (Skimming the entire assignment should be done first and a verbal review should be done after the reading is finished.)

Auxiliary Aids

ADD students may find some or all of the following to be useful.

♦ "white noise" machines

♦ earplugs

♦ daily planning calendars

♦ cognitive or self-regulatory skills such as reminders to work slowly

♦ proofreaders

♦ support groups

♦ taking an extra year to complete college

Finally, as an example, a student who has ADD and who has graduated from college has proved that accessing learning accommodations can assist individuals to perform at an academic level commensurate with their ability. After struggling for three years of college with a 2.0 grade point average, she sought help, was tested for ADD, and took untimed tests in an environment free from distractions. She raised her GPA to 3.19 and her self-esteem to "above average." She tells us that ADD is not a "life sentence," but part of a "life style" that requires some adaptations to direct her life toward achievable, realistic goals. You can do it, too.

11.

LEGAL RIGHTS OF STUDENTS WITH ADD

Peter S. Latham
and Patricia Horan Latham

ADD is a disability under federal laws when it is of sufficient severity to substantially limit a major life activity such as learning, employment, socialization, or parenting. What rights does the ADD college student have to the help that he or she needs, and what is the origin of those rights?

The rights of ADD individuals—as college students—stem basically from three sources: 1) the Constitution; 2) statutes and regulations that prohibit discrimination; and 3) cases decided by the courts. Each of these is discussed in this chapter.

THE CONSTITUTION

The 5th and 14th Amendments to the Constitution represent the most important source of the rights of individuals with disabilities. The 14th Amendment, which applies to the states, deals with equal protection under the laws and due process. The 5th Amendment, which applies to the federal government, contains the identical due process language and has incorporated the "equal protection" concept. Modern concepts of due process and equal protection for disabled persons evolved directly from the requirement of equal access to education. Although the states have no obligation to provide free public education, all states do provide it, and when they do, that education must be available to all (*Brown v. Board of Education* 347 U.S. 483 (1954)).

While *Brown* is cited primarily for its racial classification determination, it also stands for the proposition that the equal right to an education is a fundamental human right. The court said:

> In these days, it is doubtful that any child may reasonably be expected to succeed in life if he is denied the opportunity of an education. Such an opportunity, where the state has undertaken to provide it, is a right which must be made available to all on equal terms. (347 U.S. 483, at 493)

The equal "fundamental rights" analysis of *Brown* has been followed in landmark Constitutional cases involving the handicapped and learning disabled.

Equal protection of the law for persons with disabilities means an equal opportunity to obtain the same result, to gain the same benefit, or to reach the same level of achievement as nondisabled persons in the most integrated setting appropriate to that person's needs. However, opportunities in employment, education, housing, and other services, to be equally accessible, need not necessarily produce the identical result or level of achievement for handicapped and nonhandicapped persons.

These Constitutional requirements of due process and equal protection are made specific and uniform by statutes that are authorized by and implement these Constitutional provisions. In general, statutes do one of three things: 1) prohibit discrimination; 2) require affirmative action; or 3) provide funds for specific activities and programs. In the last case, the recipient is required to agree that it will conduct its programs without discrimination.

THE JUDICIAL SYSTEM

The American judicial system includes two types of courts: state courts and federal courts. The task of interpreting the United States Constitution is ultimately performed by the United States Supreme Court.

The activities of the government generate disputes, an enormous number of them. In order to reduce the volume of regular court litigation, and to ensure that governmental agencies are as free from judicial interference as possible, the states and the federal government have established a series of administrative procedures for each agency or program (and in a few cases, special courts) to resolve claims without the necessity of going to a regular court.

The Administrative procedures usually consist of a *hearing* supervised by an *administrative law judge* entitled to decide cases arising under a particular statute. The hearing is like a trial before a judge. Evidence is introduced. Witnesses may be presented, and cross-examination is allowed. The administrative law judge must then issue an opinion based on the evidence. In general, the decision is final unless 1) the findings of fact are not adequately supported by the evidence or 2) the ruling is incorrect as a matter of law.

Only a court has the authority to overturn an administrative determination, and it may do so only on the grounds set forth above. A claimant may not sue in court until he or she has obtained an administrative ruling, and then the reviewing court may consider only whether 1) the findings of fact are adequately supported by the evidence and 2) the ruling is incorrect as a matter of law. The legal phrase is that the claimant is required to *exhaust administrative remedies* before filing suit. These requirements apply generally to the enforcement of the statutory rights discussed below.

THREE FEDERAL STATUTES

The three statutes that affect the ADD college student are:

♦ The Rehabilitation Act of 1973 (RA) (29 U.S.C. §701 *et seq.*)

♦ The Individuals with Disabilities Education Act (IDEA) (20 U.S.C. §1400 *et seq.*) (ADA)

♦ The Americans with Disabilities Act (ADA) (42 U.S.C. §12101 *et seq.*)

These statutes serve generally as a model for state statutes. State laws may set higher standards than the federal ones; they may not set lower.

The RA prohibits discrimination in *employment* by the federal government, government contractors, and federal grant or aid recipients, and in *access* to the programs and activities conducted by them with federal funds. Most colleges receive federal funds, and, therefore, most are subject to the RA.

Under the RA, an individual with a disability is one who has a physical or mental impairment that substantially limits a major life activity. Regulations issued under the RA further define "mental impairment" as

> any mental or psychological disorder, such as mental retardation, organic brain syndrome, emotional or mental illness, and specific learning disabilities. (29 CFR §1613.702(b)(2))

This formulation appears in a great many regulations. The Rehabilitation Act applies to individuals with attention deficit disorder. In a Letter of Findings in OCR Case No. 04-90-1617 (17 Sep 90), the Department of Education Office for Civil Rights ruled that the Gaston County School District of North Carolina (which received federal funding) failed to identify, evaluate, and provide the complainant's ADD child with a free public education appropriate to his disorder and thereby violated the RA (29 U.S.C. §794).

The Individuals with Disabilities Education Act (IDEA) (20 U.S.C. §1400 *et seq.*) is best known for its provision of funds to elementary schools for the purpose of ensuring that all children with disabilities receive a "free appropriate public education" (FAPE). The Act and its implementing regulations contain definitions and reflect concepts that may affect colleges that receive federal financial assistance.

It is now well established that ADD is covered by the IDEA as well the RA. On September 16, 1991, the Department of Education's Office of Special Education and Rehabilitative Services issued a memorandum. This memorandum was signed by the Assistant Secretaries of the Office of Special Education and Rehabilitative Services, the Office of Civil Rights, and the Office of Elementary and Secondary Education. It represents the official position of the Department of Education and concludes that ADD children are covered by the IDEA and that any of the emphasized categories above can apply to them. The courts agree. The IDEA is enforced, either by itself or in combination with RA.

The Americans with Disabilities Act (42 U.S.C. §12101 *et seq.*) (ADA) was passed in July 1990 for the purpose of ending discrimination against individuals with disabilities in the area of employment, education, public accommodations, and licensing of professional and other activities. It extends the coverage of basic civil rights legislation (including the RA) to a wide range of public and private entities, including most colleges that do not receive federal assistance, relying heavily on the concepts and language used in the RA. Although ADD is not expressly covered in ADA such coverage is highly probable because the language of the RA, on which ADA is based, has been held to cover ADD.

WHAT IS DISCRIMINATION?

As stated in the Rehabilitation Act of 1973 a handicapped individual must establish that he or she:

1) is a "handicapped individual"; *and*

2) is "otherwise qualified"; *and*

3) was denied the benefit of a program "solely by reason" of the handicap; *and*

4) the individual, firm, or government agency that denied the benefit was federally funded. (*Fitzgerald v. Green Valley Area Education Agency* 589 F. Supp. 1130 (S.D. Iowa 1984))

Under the ADA, the presence of federal funding need not be shown, but the firm, governmental agency, institution, or activity must be one that is described in the Act.

The term "handicapped person" includes one with any "mental or psychological disorder" that "substantially limits" a "major life activity" such as working or learning. An "otherwise qualified" individual is one who, though handicapped, would be eligible for the program benefit, with or without a reasonable accommodation. If accommodation is needed, the institution must either provide the accommodation or justify, in detail, its refusal to provide it.

WHAT SPECIFIC ACCOMMODATIONS ARE REQUIRED?

In the course of issuing regulations prohibiting discrimination, the federal government has issued specific guidance listing specific accommodations to be provided. The basic requirement is established by regulations issued primarily under the RA:

45 CFR 84.44 **Academic adjustments.**

(a) *Academic requirements.* A recipient to which this

subpart applies shall make such modifications to its academic requirements as are necessary to ensure that such requirements do not discriminate or have the effect of discriminating, on the basis of handicap, against a qualified handicapped applicant or student.

The following are specified:

♦ Modifications to academic requirements, including "changes in the length of time permitted for the completion of degree requirements, substitution of specific courses required for the completion of degree requirements, and adaptation of the manner in which specific courses are conducted"

♦ The allowing of tape recorders in classrooms

♦ The use of methods for evaluating the achievement of handicapped students that will "best insure that the results of evaluation represent the student's achievement in the course, rather than reflecting the student's impaired sensory, manual, or speaking skills (except where such skills are the factors that the test purports to measure)"

♦ Auxiliary aids for students with impaired sensory, manual, or speaking skills, which aids may include taped texts, readers, classroom equipment adapted for use by students with manual impairments, and other such services and actions

The ADA and RA contain similar antidiscrimination requirements. The ADA does not *duplicate* the IDEA coverage. It is the IDEA that requires schools to provide a free appropriate public education and individualized education plans.

However, private institutions that offer secondary education, postsecondary education, courses of instruction for professional licensing, and courses for instruction in the acquisition of specific skills are covered.

Examinations must, where the disabled individual has a disability that "impairs sensory, manual, or speaking skills," assure that the "examination is selected and administered so as best to ensure" that the examination results

> accurately reflect the individual's aptitude or achievement level or whatever other factor the examination purports to measure, rather than reflecting the individual's impaired sensory, manual, or speaking skills (except where those skills are the factors that the examination purports to measure). (28 CFR 36.309(b)(i))

Course modifications are required. However, access to the test does not of itself mean access to the profession where there are other requirements (such as graduation from medical or law school) that must be met. The individual will still have to meet all prior requirements. Note, though, that these requirements themselves are subject to the terms of the ADA.

In short, the regulations cover high school, college, graduate school, and courses for specific skills such as obtaining a driver's license, computer operation, and many more. Quasi-public licensing authorities are also covered, under either this regulation or Title II (state and local governments).

The ADA will not have an impact on most traditional educational institutions. Almost all private educational institutions were already covered under 504 of the RA, depending on the amount and nature of the federal assistance they receive.

Certainly though, the ADA has highlighted these requirements, and colleges and graduate schools will be very careful
to make reasonable accommodations to learning disabled
students. The ADA will have a profound effect on those: 1) that
do not receive federal funds; 2) that offer training courses; and
3) that teach skills necessary to the issuance of licenses.

The likely accommodations are covered by existing regulations. Where specific accommodations are not covered, some
guidance may be found in the September 16, 1991, Memorandum of the Department of Education. It addressed the
accommodations that would be appropriate for many ADD
children. The remarkable thing about recommendations for
individuals with ADD is that they are relatively inexpensive
to create and implement.

ENFORCEMENT

How are rights under the RA, IDEA, and ADA enforced? The
RA and IDEA are enforced by civil suit either separately or in
combination with the IDEA, and (in appropriate cases) civil
rights statutes. The selection of appropriate statutes to invoke
must be made on the facts of a particular case. However, the RA
and the IDEA have been held to permit suit under this Act in
some situations (Actions, under 42 USCS §1983, for violations
of federal statutes pertaining to rights of handicapped persons,
63 ALR Fed 215).

The ADA contains various enforcement mechanisms. These
include actions by the EEOC, Justice Department, and (where
the ADA overlaps with the RA) the Department of Labor, as
well as private actions. The ADA enforcement provisions are

borrowed from the Civil Rights Act of 1964. They permit civil suits by individuals for injunctive relief, back pay, and, in some cases, other damages. Additionally, the Department of Justice on behalf of an individual can pursue fines and penalties. The ADA also encourages the use of alternative dispute resolutions (ADR), techniques such as settlement negotiations, conciliation, facilitation, mediation, fact finding, mini-trials, and arbitration to the extent they are "appropriate" and "authorized by law." Accordingly, it can be hoped that the resolution of disputes under the ADA will prove to be less time-consuming and expensive than under other statutes. Finally, 42 U.S.C. §12203 contains prohibitions against retaliation or coercion designed to prevent a person from exercising his or her rights under the Act. Attorneys' fees may be awarded to the prevailing party in such an action (42 U.S.C. §12205).

COLLEGE PRACTICES

Basically, a college student with ADD is entitled to the protection he or she needs so that access to education is not unjustifiably restricted because of disabilities.

Many colleges are seeking to meet their obligations to students with learning disabilities by the establishing of formalized modified admissions requirements and support programs. This assistance will be made available to many individuals with ADD simply because these individuals also have specific learning disabilities. Many colleges, even in the absence of accompanying specific learning disabilities, will extend the coverage of special services to address the attention deficits, writing problems, and organizational problems associated with ADD. These ADD deficits overlap to some extent with certain specific learning disabilities.

CONCLUSION

Finally, in the entire college process as in life, the law can provide the individual with ADD with the necessary tools to achieve success. The laws should be used wisely toward this end. At the same time, remember that the law cannot provide the most important support an individual with ADD may have: the dedication of a family member, teacher, or friend who believes in him or her. Value and rely on this above all.

12.

COMMONLY ASKED QUESTIONS

Patricia O. Quinn, M.D.

ABOUT MEDICATION

When should Ritalin or other medication be used?

Ritalin may be used whenever it is needed. It works the day you take it, and it does not usually affect your ADD symptoms on following days. It may be taken during the week, with weekends being a drug-free period; or, it may be taken during the school year, with a drug-free period in the summer. However, for many individuals, medications are necessary on a 12-month cycle. The combination of a long-acting form of the drug with a shorter acting form makes it possible to tailor the dosage you need for the most desirable effect.

What does it mean that Ritalin can be effective when taken in staggered doses, and yet we're also told that it doesn't stay in the body?

Ritalin works for 4–6 hours in most individuals. It is generally absorbed anywhere between 30 minutes and 90 minutes after an initial dose. A "wearing-off effect" is noted in some individuals, which means that a subsequent dose, sometimes in a slightly lower dose form, may be necessary in the afternoon or early evening to achieve the desired effect throughout the waking hours.

Is there a time-release form of Ritalin? How effective is it?

Ritalin comes in regular tablets of 5, 10, and 20 mg. There is also a 20-mg sustained-release (SR) form. This form is comparable to two 10-mg doses administered at 4-hour intervals. The SR is supposed to last 8 to 12 hours, but usually wears off before that time. Most clinicians feel that the SR form is not as effective as two doses of the regular 10-mg tablets, but it is smoother in release and does away with the need to administer a noontime dose of medication at school.

What are some of the side effects of Ritalin? Are there ever side effects with caffeine products and Ritalin?

The side effects of Ritalin are mainly appetite suppression and insomnia. The medication may also cause stomachaches and/or headaches. These are the more common ones, but rarer side effects are listed in Chapter 3. Ritalin is a stimulant and can mildly increase the heart rate and blood pressure. If it is combined with excessive caffeine intake, the heart rate can become accelerated. It can also result in nervousness and jitteriness. I usually recommend that patients on stimulants decrease their intake of caffeine for these reasons.

Are there problems with growth when you take these medications?

If lack of growth is considered a concern, altering the dosage alone is probably not sufficient and a change to another type of medication would be advisable. However, research has shown that there may only be a slight deceleration of growth during the initial years of stimulant use and that subsequent "catch-up" growth is seen, with no long-term growth suppression.

Are generic drugs as effective as name brand drugs?

Generic drugs, by nature, have a variability in absorption, pharmacologic effect, and effectiveness. Generic drugs may vary by 15% plus or minus in terms of their effects and side effects. As a result, the effectiveness of generic drugs can vary from individual to individual, and the experience that one person has with them can be surprisingly different from that with the original parent compounds. Generic methylphenidate is reported by some not to be as effective as the brand name Ritalin.

Are combinations of medicine ever prescribed? Has Zolof or Prozac been used with Ritalin?

Although combinations of medicines are used for ADHD, stimulants are still more commonly used alone. Sometimes tricyclic antidepressants are used in place of or in addition to stimulants, especially if other symptoms, such as depression or severe impulse problems, are present. Prozac is sometimes used in combination with Ritalin.

When should stimulants and when should antidepressants be used to get students through school?

Stimulants are usually used if the diagnosis is ADHD *and* the student can take stimulants without uncomfortable side effects. For those who cannot take stimulant medications, tricyclic antidepressants are often used. Some doctors feel that the tricyclics are not quite as good at controlling attention, but they do seem to work nonetheless. For students with depression symptoms as well as ADHD, an antidepressant may be the best choice. Medical monitoring is necessary.

Do I have to take Ritalin for the rest of my life?

Not necessarily. The hyperactive symptoms are the symptoms most likely to diminish with age. Many students learn to exert better control over attention and impulses as they get older, but high school and college students may choose to continue the use of medication for academic pursuits. Some adults decide to resume the use of medication to help with attention span. Medications, in fact, work just as well with adults with ADHD as they do with ADHD children!

ABOUT
TREATMENT PROGRAMS

Are support groups helpful for people with ADD?

Absolutely! It really helps to know that you are not alone and to learn from your peers what *they* do to deal with ADD.

Trained group leaders can suggest resources that can be very helpful, including resources for college planning.

ABOUT COLLEGE ADMISSION AND SATs

What do you need for diagnosis/permission to take untimed SATs?

The current Educational Testing Service (ETS) requirements for eligibility to take untimed SATs are that a student must have *on file at his or her school* either a current Individualized Education Program (IEP) or *two* signed documents, based on 1990–1994 test results, obtained from any of the following: physician(s), psychologist(s), child-study team(s), or learning-disability specialist(s). Both documents cannot be from the same individual or team.

The IEP must state the nature and effect of the disability and the need for modified testing arrangements.

The two signed documents must state and describe the disability, the tests used in diagnosis, and the need for special testing arrangements. In addition, *these signed documents must affirm that the disability meets state guidelines for certification when such guidelines exist.*

Will a "nonstandard administration" SAT label (when taken untimed) negatively affect the university's acceptance decision?

Students who choose to take the untimed SATs are not discriminated against in the college admissions process.

What else can students with ADD do to improve chances of admission to colleges when their academic profile is not "stellar"?

Students who do not have a stellar academic profile need to set up a personal interview with an admissions officer in order to explain *in person* circumstances that may have affected their school record.

How recent does testing documenting learning disabilities have to be?

Typically, colleges with learning support programs require testing to be completed within two years prior to the application.

How can I find out which schools offer special services?

There isn't any simple formula for discovering colleges with learning support programs. Many college guides identify colleges with support. After reviewing the available literature, visiting the campus and meeting with a staff member of the support program is the best approach.

ABOUT PARENT INVOLVEMENT

How involved should parents be when ADD students look at colleges?

Students need to feel that they will be attending a college of their choice. Parents can help by providing guidance and support with research, establishing parameters on which to base a decision (i.e., defining criteria for creating a short list), and articulating constraints that they feel as parents are relevant (e.g., financial, geographic). The most important thing is to be available for consultation and advice, when invited, and to encourage such interaction.

ABOUT
LEARNING ACCOMMODATIONS

What kinds of support do colleges provide?

As discussed in Chapter 10, colleges offer varying levels of support. A college may be listed as providing services or a program for learning-disabled students, or it may have both. Colleges with programs for learning-disabled students generally have more comprehensive supports for students with learning disabilities and ADD than do colleges with just service models.

Are classroom adaptations such as laptop computers, scribes, or recordings for the blind helpful to the student with ADD?

Classroom adaptations can help students with ADD to compensate for their high level of distractibility. If, for example, the student is subject to a high level of noise distraction, augmenting the reading process with relevant auditory stimuli can result in a more accurate understanding of reading requirements.

How can a student best become his or her own advocate to receive needed services?

A student can become his or her own advocate by understanding his or her individual disability from the perspective of his or her learning profile. The student should advocate by explaining personal strengths and weaknesses and proposing alternative assignments and/or exams that would enable him or her to demonstrate actual academic capability.

Will schools schedule classes in accordance with ADD students' sleeping habits and needs for concentration?

In general, schools schedule classes from 8:00 a.m. to 10:40 p.m. Students with ADD must choose the most appropriate times to meet their own needs. It is important to work closely with an academic advisor, looking at all the requirements for the student's major, and determining ahead of time if classes can be taken during a later semester or during summer session. Frequently, schools with programs for learning-disabled students also have special advisors who help with this. Students also need to be realistic about what scheduling they can manage. Don't take an 8:30 a.m. class if you can't get up to attend the class.

Does reduced course work affect financial aid?

Reduced course work *can* affect financial aid, but again, this depends on the school itself. It is important that this question be explored at the time of application.

ABOUT LEGAL ISSUES

Are legal accommodations for college students different than for high school students?

The obligation to provide accommodations at the college level, as a practical matter, is similar to that at the high school level. However, there are differences in the statutory requirements applicable to each. See Chapter 11 for more details.

References for Information about Adolescents and Adults with ADD

BOOKS

Attention Deficit Disorder in Adults: Support and Practical Help for Sufferers and Their Spouses, by Lynn Weiss. Rochester, MI: Taylor Publishing, 1991.

Hyperactive Children Grown Up: Empirical Findings and Theoretical Considerations, by Gabrielle Weiss and Lily T. Hechtman. New York: Guilford Press, 1986.

The Hyperactive Child, Adolescent, and Adult: Attention Deficit Disorder Through the Lifespan, by Paul H. Wender. New York: Oxford University Press, 1987.

COLLEGE GUIDES

The K & W Guide to Colleges for the Learning Disabled, edited by Marybeth Kravets and Imy F. Wax. New York: Harper Collins, 1992.

Peterson's Guide to Colleges with Programs for Students with Learning Disabilites, edited by Charles T. Mangrum, III and Stephen S. Strichart. Princeton, NJ: Petersons Guides, 1992.

Unlocking Potential: College and Other Choices for Learning Disabled People—A Step-by-Step Guide, by Barbara Scheiber and Jeanne Talpers. Chevy Chase, MD: Adler & Adler, 1987.

NEWSLETTERS

ADDendum (for Adults Who Have ADD), edited by Paul Jaffee, c/o CPS, 5041A Backlick Road, Annandale, VA 22003.

ADDult News, quarterly newsletter, 2620 Ivy Place, Toledo, OH 43613.

Challenge, Inc., ADDA newsletter, P.O. Box 488, West Newbury, MA 01985.

CH.A.D.D.ER, 499 N.W. 70th Avenue, Suite 308, Plantation, FL 33317.

ORGANIZATIONS

ADDA, National Attention Deficit Disorders Association, 19262 Jamboree Road, Irvine, CA 92715.

ADDult Support Network, 2620 Ivy Place, Toledo, OH 43613. This organization also offers an information packet and a pen pal service.

CHADD, a nonprofit parent-based organization for individuals with ADD, 499 N.W. 70th Avenue, Suite 308, Plantation, FL 33317; 305-587-3700.

Appendix:
Definitions of ADHD

In order for you to further understand both the symptoms and the diagnosis of ADHD, the following proposed definitions of the American Psychiatric Association and the American Academy of Pediatrics are provided.

AMERICAN PSYCHIATRIC ASSOCIATION
DSM-IV DRAFT DIAGNOSTIC CRITERIA FOR
ATTENTION-DEFICIT/HYPERACTIVITY DISORDER*

A. Either (1) or (2):
   (1) Inattention: At least six of the following symptoms of inattention have persisted for at least six months to a degree that is maladaptive and inconsistent with developmental level:
      (a) often fails to give close attention to details or makes careless mistakes in schoolwork, work, or other activities
      (b) often has difficulty sustaining attention in tasks or play activities
      (c) often does not seem to listen to what is being said to him or her
      (d) often does not follow through on instructions and fails to finish schoolwork, chores, or duties in the workplace (not due to oppositional behavior or failure to understand instructions)
      (e) often has difficulties organizing tasks and activities

---

*Permission to reprint from DSM-IV Draft Criteria 3/1/93 granted by the American Psychiatric Association. © 1993 by the American Psychiatric Association.

    (f) often avoids, expresses reluctance about, or has difficulties engaging in tasks that require sustained mental effort (such as schoolwork or homework)

    (g) often loses things necessary for tasks or activities (e.g., school assignments, pencils, books, tools, or toys)

    (h) is often easily distracted by extraneous stimuli

    (i) often forgetful in daily activities

(2) Hyperactivity-impulsivity: At least five of the following symptoms of hyperactivity-impulsivity have persisted for at least six months to a degree that is maladaptive and inconsistent with developmental level:

Hyperactivity

    (a) often fidgets with hands or feet or squirms in seat

    (b) leaves seat in classroom or in other situations in which remaining seated is expected

    (c) often runs about or climbs excessively in situations where it is inappropriate (in adolescents or adults, may be limited to subjective feelings of restlessness)

    (d) often has difficulty playing or engaging in leisure activities quietly

    (e) is always "on the go" or acts as if "driven by a motor"

    (f) often talks excessively

Impulsivity

    (g) often blurts out answers to questions before the questions have been completed

    (h) often has difficulty waiting in lines or awaiting turn in games or group situations

    (i) often interrupts or intrudes on others (e.g., butts into other's conversations or games)

B. Some symptoms that caused impairment were present before age seven.

C. Some symptoms that cause impairment are present in two or more settings (e.g., at school, work, and at home).

D. There must be clear evidence of clinically significant impairment in social, academic, or occupational functioning.

E. Does not occur exclusively during the course of a Pervasive

Developmental Disorder, Schizophrenia or other Psychotic Disorder, and is not better accounted for by a Mood Disorder, Anxiety Disorder, Dissociative Disorder, or a Personality Disorder.

Code based on type:

314.00 **Attention-deficit/Hyperactivity Disorder, Predominantly Inattentive Type:** if criterion A(1) is met but not criterion A(2) for the past six months

314.01 **Attention-deficit/Hyperactivity Disorder, Predominantly Hyperactive-Impulsive Type:** if criterion A(2) is met but not criterion A(1) for the past six months

314.01 **Attention-deficit/Hyperactivity Disorder, Combined Type:** if both criteria A(1) and A(2) are met for the past six months

Coding note: for individuals (especially adolescents and adults) who currently have symptoms that no longer meet full criteria, "in partial remission" should be specified.

AMERICAN ACADEMY OF PEDIATRICS DEFINITION OF ADHD*
(Response to Department of Education Notice of Inquiry—March 1991)

The disorders known as Attention-Deficit Hyperactivity Disorders (ADHDs) are chronic neurological conditions resulting from persisting dysfunction within the central nervous system and manifesting symptoms referred to as dysfunctions of selective attention, impulse control, executive functions in controlling cognitive tasks, motor activity, and social interaction. Such symptoms are often seen in

---

*Used with permission from the American Academy of Pediatrics: Response to Dept. of Education's request for written comments on special education under the Individuals With Disabilities Education Act (Part B) for children with attention deficit disorders.

association with disorders of learning, cognitive processing, memory, sequencing, motor skills, receiving or expressing language, and central processing of sensory information. The symptoms must be significant and continuous over time."

Operational characteristics for each of the seven types of dysfunction:

1. Selective Focus of Attention may be shown by an easy distractibility from sights and sounds ubiquitous in an educational environment, by overfocusing on activities and then being unable to disengage from them, or being unable to select the most appropriate stimulus or individual to be attended to in the educational setting. A child may demonstrate similar behaviors outside the classroom.

2. Impulsivity may be demonstrated by the inability to think of an action without performing the motor act, by being easily susceptible to other children's suggestions for inappropriate behaviors, or by being unable to resist immediate action from internally stimulated desires.

3. Motoric restlessness must be documented by different mechanisms at differing ages of the child; driven, highly overactive behavior in a young child, or excessive fidgeting, squirming, fighting behaviors in a school-aged child may serve as appropriate age-differentiating symptoms.

4. Difficulty interpreting social cues might be operationally diagnosed through the child's inability to recognize common social signals communicated from other people ("lack of a social antenna"), by not knowing when to stop activities in response to the feelings others express, or by not recognizing signals of approval or disapproval from teachers or peers.

5. Executive functioning disorders may be recognized by difficulty planning, organizing, or performing tasks sequentially, appropriately starting or stopping suitable activities, inhibiting activity where appropriate, or difficulty shifting from one activity to another.

CAMBRIA COUNTY LIBRARY
JOHNSTOWN, PA. 15901

6. Reduced self-monitoring may be recognized by the inability to recognize what has been done, by not recognizing success or failure in task performance or social setting or by failing to check performance prior to initiating new tasks.
7. Low frustration tolerance may be demonstrated by the development of socially unacceptable behaviors when the child is unable to attain desired goals or perform expected tasks.